the TRAVEL BOG diaries

One Woman's wickedly funny confessions
of surviving family travel

LIZ DEACLE

The Travel Bog Diaries

All Rights Reserved

COPYRIGHT © 2023 Liz Deacle

ISBN: 978-1-7385920-0-5

Cover design: L1graphics.

Edited by Hilary Jastram

DEDICATION

For my three. And for Mum. Without whom, none of this would've been possible. I love you.

GET IN TOUCH

www.lizdeacle.com

TABLE OF CONTENTS

Please assume all names and places have been changed. Not to protect the innocent but because my brain is like a sieve, so I make random stuff up. The same goes for any important-sounding facts. Take it all with a pinch of salt. Preferably the pink Himalayan stuff, it's better for you. Thank you for your understanding. I blame my age. Although my husband says I have always been like this.

Wait … I have a husband?

INTRODUCTION

I was always desperate to be a yummy mummy. A yommy mommy. A yamma mama.

One of those parents who jogged effortlessly through the park wearing lip-gloss and a baseball cap. Pushing a baby in a three-wheeler pram. Never getting the wheels stuck in a drain. Never leaking urine from her pelvic floor.

But sadly, it seemed the mummy fairy had me pegged for different things. *Cow.*

After the birth of my son in 2001, who was born three weeks early (and arrived carrying a fistful of my poo), followed three years later by my daughter, who sprang into the world via Concorde (leaving me traumatised for what seemed like years), it was obvious, that my mothering experience would be far from yummy.

Scummy, funny, bummy, money (zapping), shunny, cummy (ahem), runny, sunny, but never it seemed, yummy. Not me. Not today. Not ever.

Move along the fairy line, please.

There are two kinds of women in this world. The woman who shows up at the airport wearing a white vest and oversized grey track pants, and the woman who shows up at the airport wearing a white vest and oversized grey track pants.

It's a trick. They look the same but are entirely different. I blame the mama fairy. She's sick and twisted and probably has mental issues.

The first woman at the airport wears the outfit because an hour earlier, she peeled herself from her Italian lover's silk-sheeted bed and, after realising she had a flight to catch, quickly snatched his gym pants from the bathroom floor and paired them with the dinky white vest she'd slept in the night before. The one that smells of sex and cigarettes.

The other woman wears the same outfit because it is day twenty-two of her cycle. She has so much water retention, her belly resembles that of a pregnant hippopotamus. The stretchy size 20 pants she bought from Primark (in the sale) are ideal for this long flight. And the white sleeveless vest? It's made of thick non-see-through cotton, meaning that when she goes to the bathroom an hour into the flight to take off her bra, she can do so without fear of her giant brown nipples being spotted by the air hostess, who would most certainly scream hysterically and throw herself out of the cockpit window.

Hello. I'm Liz. Woman number two. Lover of free-swinging breasts and advocate of baggy pants.

As I enter my fifth decade, I have resigned myself to the fact that I never was, have been or *will be* a dazzling diva who drinks cocktails in the bath. I buy daily contact lenses and make them last two weeks by spitting on them. I still wear my ugly-but-comfy high-waisted "time of the month" knickers to bed every night, even though my periods stopped a year ago, and though it shames me to admit this, sometimes…I wee in the bath.

My life is quite messy. I balance my time between training my lip not to quiver while watching blind donkey videos and fantasising about achieving unattainable goals. Sometimes my family worries about me. They suspect I am either a: on the verge of a nervous breakdown or b: a drug addict. Neither is true, of course. I'm just discovering myself is all. Exploring my emotions. Deep diving. Growing. In all directions.

Take writing this book, for instance.

If you'd told me two years ago that I'd be piecing together an introduction for a book I'd written, I'd have shaken my head and snorted. Not in front of you because I'm British and British people aren't rude. Nor do they grunt like pigs. No. I'd have waited for you to leave the room and done it behind your back.

*The Brits are all closet snobs and are hideously two-faced. It's in our blood. I think it stems back to when Henry was king, and he couldn't get his end away with Anne Boleyn.

'A book? Me?' I'd have cried. 'I don't think so. I don't even know the difference between a real comma and one of those with a dot above it'. *(True fact.)*

Yet here I am. Writing a book. Talking to you. With newly acquired knowledge from Google that the comma with the dot above it is called a semi-colon and is used when you want the reader to pause but not fall asleep.

There are lots of other things in life I assumed I'd never be able to do. Some of which I did and some I'm still working on. Giving birth twice without going to a hospital. (Yes.) Teaching my kids from home instead of sending them to school. (Yes.) Getting on the front page of *Home and Garden*. (As if.) Travelling the world for a year with two teenagers and a husband with an acid reflux problem. (Yes.)

I'll say that again, in case you missed it the first time.

'Travelling the world for a year with two teenagers and a husband with an acid reflux problem. YES'.

I know. I still can't believe I'm talking about myself when I say that out loud—me, of all people.

You see ...

Up until a few years ago, I believed that people *like us, like me and you,* don't do things like travel the world. No. People like us sit on the toilet scrolling Pinterest. Wishing we owned an outdoor pizza oven and a pergola with fairy lights. People like us make to-do lists and add things we've already completed so we can cross them off and feel instant gratification.

People like us *don't* turn our backs on everyday life and take our kids travelling around the world for a year.

Not us. No way. Uhh uh.

Anyway, even if we wanted to up and leave, how could we? We're not millionaires. Or missionaries. We're certainly not influencers (whatever that stupid word means). People like us don't build orphanages or eat mung bean stew. We don't even know what language they speak in India.

Is it Hindu, or is that a religion??

People like us stay at home. With our phone-addicted kids. And our kitchen drawer filled with lidless plastic containers. And our yappy dog that has separation anxiety.

People like us don't leave everything behind and take off around the world for a year. They just DON'T. The end.

Do they?

Yes.

Apparently, they do.

After years of being the woman who spent hours devouring social media posts about families who went on exotic trips for a really long time, I finally did the same. Me and my family. We went around the world. We upped, took off and went. Just like that. No experience, no previous convictions. Nothing.

We sold my husband's business and used the proceeds of the sale ($50,000 that had been allocated for our retirement) to travel around the world for a year. We left our house, car, clothes, the kids' friends, school work, *and* our nervous dog and swapped it for three hundred and sixty-five glorious (mostly glorious) days trotting around the globe.

How you came to be holding a book written by me. *Crikey.*

It was never my intention to write a book. I fell into it. Tripped. Wobbled. Tumbled in true messy fashion.

Before we left for our year away, I started a blog. We needed money, I had a second-hand laptop, and we were about to travel the world.

Why not build a business around travel? Become a travel blogger. Earn on the go. Easy peasy!

In my mind, I was going to be famous. Make my millions by writing for fancy travel magazines and big-page newspapers. But things didn't quite go to plan. Finding an internet café and reporting on why you should buy a suitcase with wheels was boring. I was far happier taking myself off to a quiet toilet and scribbling down the toe-curling things that happened to my family and me on a daily basis.

Cringey things. Embarrassing things. The kind of things that normal people keep to themselves.

Like what it feels like when you piss your pants two minutes before boarding a train in Sri Lanka.

The year we backpacked the world as a family was the best of our lives. Well, it was certainly mine. I can't speak for the kids. When we returned home from our trip, they took to their room and haven't emerged since. They're still in there. Three years later. Banging their heads against the wall and muttering.

We made so many gorgeous memories. Did things that we never thought we were capable of. We Couchsurfed (I'll tell you more about that later) all over the world. Slept on sleeper buses in India. Spent Christmas in New York. Read books beneath cherry trees in Japan.

And all on a budget no bigger than a tea-leaf.

Never has there been (or probably will there ever be) a season in my life when I felt so utterly grateful every single day. Filled with joy to be wrapped in the arms of my beautiful family. Entwined by adventure. Bound by experiences.

It was glorious! It was magnificent!

But here's the thing.

Before we left for this trip, I did masses of research. Not the kind of research I should have been doing, like what happens when you miss the last train in Tokyo. No. I scoured bookstores, blogs and went on every social media platform I could find, looking for scraps of evidence from families who had done what we were about to do. I wanted reassurance. Someone to tell me that although travelling might not always be pretty, it would be okay. That we'd survive.

And there were plenty. Of families, I mean. Unbeknownst to me, lots of parents take their kids and travel the globe together. *Perfect! My search was over!*

But there was just one problem.

Every piece of information I found told only of the good times. The triumphs that these travelling families had experienced. The perfectness and the jolliness and the poppetness of it all.

Look at us!! We're all so happy! Our kids spend their days chatting with world leaders while we milk goats with our toes!

Not once did the mum say, '*When you get to Sri Lanka, be warned. They have this wood apple juice, and it makes you shit bricks*'. Or, '*Oh, yes. Italy's lovely, but the bottled water in Rome is a complete rip-off. You won't be able to afford it, which means you'll all be dehydrated, cranky and hate each other's guts by the time you make it to the Pantheon*'.

So.

While I could very well share tender, marvellous, fantabulous stories of how I patted my son's head in Ireland and smiled on adoringly because he bravely forwent his fear of spiders so his sister could have the big bed, I know you'd be bored stiff by page three.

What you have here is the opposite of what most other travellers share. You're going to be let in on a few family secrets.

Just whatever you do, don't tell my kids what this book is about. They think I've spent the last two years writing a dissertation on the intricacies of Victorian water closets.

The stories you are about to read were written from the seats of various lavatories. Secluded toilets in far-flung corners of the world. Peaceful places where I would hide, hunched over, alone. Furiously pencilling down the details of what it *really* means to be a globetrotting family.

These notes affectionately became known as the *Bog Diaries*. Whenever I disappeared, the kids would say, 'Oh, she's probably writing her travel BOG'. ("Bog" being an English slang word for toilet), and then they'd roll around in fits of laughter.

I know. *Cruel bastards.*

Needless to say, I never made a living from being a travel blogger. Not a cent. But I did return home with a fist full of stories. True stories from around the world. And those stories are hidden in the book that you are now holding.

Don't worry. I wipe front to back, and I *always* wash my hands.

This book is not your average family travel guide. I wish it were; then my kids would be able to read it without dying of embarrassment. But it isn't. You are about to discover what happens when an ordinary family does something extraordinary. You'll get the truth, the whole truth and nothing but the you-probably-should-have-kept-that-to-yourself truth.

Because as much as I'd like you to believe that I am a cool Instagramable hippie-chick who floated around the world in her long white cheesecloth dress, giggling with her hunky husband and tickling the cheeks of her adorable (and very intelligent) teenagers; wondering together at all the wondrous wonders of the wonderful world. The truth was quite the opposite.

The only thing my son wondered about was why the Wi-Fi was so shit in Columbo.

But do not despair. While I might not be able to tell you how to get from Washington to Warsaw on the back of a water buffalo, I can offer you something far more valuable.

Inspiration.

After reading this book, it is my hope that you will feel inspired to have an adventure of your own. Because up until last week, I didn't even know that Ireland was part of the United Kingdom. And I lived in England for forty-eight years. Seriously. If I can do it, anyone can.

While I'm at it, I also hope you'll share my book with millions of your friends. So I can finally afford Botox. Thanks in advance.

That's it! The introductions are done. It's time to board the flight and get on with our trip. Sit back, enjoy the ride and for God's sake, don't slop wine down your grey trackie pants.

You didn't keep the receipt. Remember?

CHAPTER ONE
A FAMILY OF FOUR

Ten days. Ten measly days. That's all the holiday we could take. Any longer than that, and my husband's business would collapse. Or worse still, his head would explode, leaving me and the kids destitute and without a daddy. And no one wants that. Not when the filter on the water softener still needs replacing.

I'd be lying if I said I wasn't bitter. About the holiday-length thing, I mean. I was. This wasn't what I'd been promised. I'd been ripped off. Tricked. Led up the garden path.

Blimey, listen to me, blabbing on! Chewing your ear off when we've only just met. Where's my manners? I haven't even introduced myself properly or told you about Brian and the kids. Or how we went from being a (semi) normal family who only ever took an annual ten-day camping trip to four very savvy backpackers who hot-footed around the globe on a shoestring and managed to (just about) survive.

Brian

First, you should know about Brian. Brian is my husband. We met at a nightclub in our hometown of Newquay (England's answer to Ibiza) back in 1988. I was seventeen with a flicked fringe and ripped jeans, and he was twenty-six with a moustache and a Ford Escort van. Brian was a plumber who also dabbled in a bit of local DJ-ing on the side. When he wasn't screwing pipes and greasing back-flows, he was turning the tables and spinning the discs.

Tooting the tunes like a good 'un.

One night, me and a friend went along to the club where Brian was working (this was before checking IDs was a thing—when all you had to do to get in anywhere illegal was stick your boobs out and pout at the bouncers.) We were standing at the bar sipping on our fifty-pence lime and sodas when our favourite song blasted through the speakers.

'Nah, nah, nah nah nananana, oo-ooh'.

'Oh my GOD, this song is so RAD!' I shouted in my friend's ear, gulping back mouthfuls of that foggy dense vapour that makes nightclubs look so cool. 'Let's DANCE!' We rushed to the flashing neon floor excitedly, dropping our handbags between us and dancing around them.

And that's when I heard it. For the very first time.

The voice of my future husband.

'I bet this girl doesn't need to get naked to have a good time', murmured Brian into the microphone. Then he stood back and flashed me a wink and a smile.

I know. Bit corny, isn't it?

But back then, I didn't think so. I actually really liked it. Even though I blushed and made out that I was embarrassed, secretly, I was flattered and relished the attention. You have to remember that this was the 1980s. In the days before clingfilm was deemed evil, and the telly only had four channels. When women enjoyed flirting with men. If you'd asked someone back then what invasion of personal space meant, they probably would have told you it was the title of the new *Star Wars* film.

I was completely won over by Brian's sexy Liverpudlian accent and the fact that he looked a bit like Barry from *Brookside*, so when he asked me to go for a cup of tea with him the next day, I readily agreed.

Everyone said it wouldn't last. Brian was eight years older than me, and we had very different interests. What on earth could a plumber-slash-vinyl jock have in common with an extremely sophisticated (and a bit up her own arse) A-level drama student?

But we continued to date, me and Bri.

Driving around Cornwall in his little white van. Camping in woods and lighting fires (we weren't pyromaniacs or anything, we just got a bit chilly). We'd walk along the Cornish cliffs and talk for hours, eat picnics and watch the sunset over the Atlantic Ocean.

It was all very romantic.

Once, we even pretended that we were Baby and Johnny and took pictures of each other straddling a wet log. When the photos came back from Boots, I wrote across one of them using my best gold tip marker. The words said, "My love is yours. So don't ever put me in the corner." Then I scribbled "Peace" underneath and signed my name with a love heart over the *i*.

I gave the photo to Brian as a gift. He was delighted. He placed his hand on his hairy chest. Let out a small weep. I stroked his arm tenderly and reminded him that I had a B minus in English Literature. And that if we were to stay together he would have to accept that his girlfriend was an incredibly deep and poetic artist.

The years passed, and the teenage romance morphed into something more serious. I loved Brian, and he loved me, and twelve years after that night on the dance floor, we exchanged marriage vows in a quaint church in the middle of the English countryside.

I couldn't have been happier. I had the man of my dreams. By my side forever.

Our lives from there melted into one big beautiful blur of travel, houses, babies, emigrating and homeschooling (which I'll tell you about later). And now here we are, thirty-odd years and two kids later. Living on the other side of the world in New Zealand. Me and the Scouse plumber. Hopelessly devoted to each other.

Like Sandy and Danny but without the ciggies and the flying car.

The kids

I know you're not supposed to write about your family and put it out into the world for everyone and their dog to see, but this book revolves around my kids, so I don't have much choice.

I could always change their names, I suppose, but that might get confusing.

Anyway, I'll only forget what I'm doing and mess it up.

Like that time when I worked as a waitress for a high-end catering agency in London back in the early nineties. There was this super posh event, red carpet and everything. Masses of music moguls wearing expensive suits gathered on a rooftop bar to fawn over some band whose latest album had won an award. My job was easy. All I had to do was walk around and fill empty glasses. Keep my smile fixed, my eyes down and under NO circumstances address any of the band members by name.

Everything was going spiffingly until I realised that the man standing to my left was the same man who I sang along with every Christmas in the record section of Woolworths. I was fired on the spot after hovering over him, totally starstruck with a bottle of champagne fizzing all over my hand, gushing: 'Top up, Bono?'

No. I won't change my kids' names. Best not.

Before I introduce you to my darling children, there is something I need to say. A disclaimer. My kids mean the world to me. Just so you know. And while you might hear me say lots of horrid and wicked things about them in this book, I actually love them. A lot.

A big lot.

Right. That's that sorted.

Let the tongue wagging commence.

Sonny

First up is my son, Sonny. Sixteen. Lanky. Goofy. Spotty. Phone addict. Joker. Cheeky. Handsome. A God. Can do no wrong. Worshipped by everyone. Especially me.

If I had one wish, it would be to freeze time and keep Sonny just as he is now. Like Peter Pan. So he would live at home and never move away, and we could spend our nights together, flying around the city, soaring over moonlit buildings, and oohing and aahing at the twinkly stars.

Me and my boy. Together forever.

Him in his green tights and feather cap and me in my flannelette Wendy nightie and baggy knickers.

I haven't told him this yet, I'm waiting for the right moment, but if he ever gets a girlfriend, I'll find a really deep well and then chuck her down it.

Push. Splash. Gone. Bye, bye tweetheart. Must fly.

Unless, of course, she's an orphan looking for a mother figure. In which case, I'll lock her in our spare room and only let her out at Christmas.

Tessa

My daughter, Tessa. Thirteen. Kind. Gentle. Homebody. Worry wort. Easily frustrated. Brilliant. Talented. Patient. Loves her dad the most, and he loves her back. But not as much as I love her. All my life, I dreamt of having a daughter, and along she came.

She is everything I wish I were.

If I had my way, Tessa would be kept in a tall ivory tower for the rest of her life. So I could spend my days singing lullabies to her and making daisy chains for her to wear in her really long hair.

When the time comes for *her* to get a boyfriend or girlfriend (have to be careful here, she's very politically correct and hates it when I show ignorance), I'll dress up in a bunny suit and dance around the garden with a knife between my teeth. Yes... that should do it…Either that or I'll put said person in the bedroom with Sonny's girlfriend and hope they fall in love and escape together.

And then there's me. Liz.

An average mum, married to an extraordinary man, living with two wonderful but typically annoying teenagers.

A woman who pees when she laughs and cries when she looks at old baby photos. A woman who loves wine a little too much. Who, more than once, has poured the entire bottle of her favourite Merlot into a plastic measuring jug and then topped up her glass to see exactly how much over the standard recommendations she is guzzling every night.

Liz. A woman who isn't ready to get old.

Who longs to go hot air ballooning in Turkey and ride camels in the Indian desert (even though she's terrified of heights and can't straddle a bike without bringing on a nasty bout of cystitis).

Liz. A woman who, despite the fact that up until last month, thought that the Terracotta Army was some sort of Nazi religious camp in Texas, chose to be brave. To do the thing she'd always dreamed of doing. To take her family and travel the world.

Okay. All up to date. Back to the story. Oh, no, wait. Hang on. There's one more thing I should mention. It's about the c-word.

The Change.

Since entering mid-life, I have suffered from terrible brain fog. It makes me forget things. Go off on a tangent. Lose my place. Which is not ideal when you're trying to write a book. But don't worry. The HRT is working wonders.

I just need to remember which day to change the sodding patch.

CHAPTER TWO
LET'S JUST GO

R emember in the last chapter when I told you we were only ever able to take ten days annual leave? Well, now I'm going to share why. But before I do, we need to go back a few years. A decade to be exact.

It wasn't Brian's fault.

He was just trying to put food on the table and pay the mortgage. We'd built our home a year earlier and had made use of his many skills. Which was great because it meant we didn't have to pay any tradesmen but not great because we weren't getting a wage from the job. The house had taken sixteen months to complete. Our credit cards were through the roof. Brian was now officially unemployed.

'I think I should go into business with Sam', Brian blurted out one afternoon. It was a damp Autumn day. Grey and blustery. We were walking our dog, Maggie, on the beach, trying to tire her out so she wouldn't go into the garden and dig up the crocus bulbs I'd spent ages planting. 'Installing heating systems'. He swallowed and waited.

I'll admit the conversation took me by surprise. The last time we'd spoken, everything seemed fine. The plan was that he'd complete the last bits and pieces on the property. Tie up the loose ends. As far as I knew, he was to be staining the outside of the new shed in Deep Oak.

I reached into Maggie's mouth and pried out the stone she had clamped between her back teeth.

Annoyingly our dog chews rocks. Don't ask me why; I have no idea. The vet said it probably has something to do with me homeschooling the kids—that she felt abandoned at a crucial time in her puppy development, and it's given her some sort of anxiety issues. What a load of crap. *(Obviously, I would never say that out loud as vets have been to university and are clever and rich.)* All I know is anxiety or no anxiety, chewing rocks causes my dog's teeth to fall out, which in turn leads to a vet visit, which in turn leads to him making me feel bad for home-educating my sprogs.

'No, Maggie! NO. Naughty!' I wagged my finger and hid the stone behind my back. She danced on her back legs and chattered her teeth. I turned to Brian.

'Sorry, who? Sam? What, Scottish Sam? The same Sam who six months ago you said was dodgy, and you couldn't believe he'd got his license passed?'

The wind from the sea whipped around our legs. We lowered our heads and fell into a slow, determined pace.

'I didn't say he was dodgy, Liz. I said he was podgy. And that's only because his wife works in the bakery and brings home the leftover pies. And I never said that about the license either; that was someone else. Sam's a bloody good tradie'. He threw a stick for Maggie.

Hmm. I wasn't sure.

We'd only ever done things together, Brian and me. As a team. We'd run a ski chalet in Canada, owned a café back in the nineties, bought and sold eight properties, and, most recently, emigrated from England to New Zealand. The plan was after we'd finished building our home, we'd start something new. Together. And that time was now. But… money was tight, and I'd recently committed to homeschooling our kids. So our plan wasn't realistic. Or feasible. And Brian being Brian, was looking out for us. Securing our future.

I knew he was right, but still, I couldn't help feeling abandoned. Dumped. Jealous.

'I don't know', I said, dragging my foot in the sand sullenly. 'What if this Sam does us over and runs off with all the money? Or worse still, tries to get us into swinging? That's what business partners do, isn't it? Get all chummy-chummy and then sleep with each other's wives'.

Brian turned to face me and forced out a I-can't-believe-you-actually-just-said-that laugh.

'His wife is up to her neck in dough all day, Liz. The last thing she's thinking about is asking us over for a shag'.

I frowned. I don't like men who use coarse language.

We fell back into step. Brian pressed on.

'I think this partnership will really benefit us. It means we'll start earning some decent money and, more importantly, because there'll be two of us running the show, we can take time off. At least a month at a time'.

So the deal was done.

The papers were signed, and give Brian his due; in the first year of the partnership, we went to California with the kids for a month. That holiday was fabulous, but (for reasons I won't go into here) when we returned home to New Zealand, the business was close to tatters. Jobs were backed up, customers were complaining, and due to the stress of being left alone to organise a team of rowdy apprentices, Sam had turned to comfort eating. Scoffing pies like they were going out of fashion.

'I'm never doing that again', huffed Brian, fraught and anxious, his Californian tan fading in front of my eyes. 'It's not worth it. It's clear that this business needs two people here. At. All. Times'.

So that was that.

The "more time" promise disintegrated, and for seven years, we never left New Zealand. Our family holidays (or "vacations" as they say in America) were spent three hours from home. On a campsite. A very nice campsite, I might add, but still … a campsite. Where we only ever stayed for ten days. No more. No less.

Until one night …

They say everyone can remember significant dates in their lives, don't they? Like when Kennedy was shot or Elvis died. I don't know anyone who can't recall what they were doing when Diana climbed out of her Cinderella carriage and walked up the aisle to marry two-timing Charles.

I remember the exact minute we decided to change our lives and throw everything up in the air to travel the world. Me, Brian, and the kids. For a *whole year*.

We were camping at Blue Lake in Rotorua on the North Island of New Zealand. We'd spent the day at Kerosene Creek, a nearby popular tourist spot famous for its idyllic hot pools. On our way back to the car, we got chatting with a bunch of young backpackers, buzzing with energy and youthfulness as they shared the places they'd been and adventures that lay ahead. They were so carefree and joyful (as is the case when you're twenty and think your tummy will always be that flat and you'll never get tonsil stones or piles).

That night, outside the tent, feeling warm and relaxed, Brian and I drank wine and chatted about our day. We reflected on our conversation with the backpackers and agreed their enthusiasm was magnetic. As the stars grew brighter and the wine loosened our tongues, we fantasized about what it would be like to travel the world with our kids.

Where would we go? What would we do? How long would we go for? How much money would we need?

This wasn't a new topic of conversation for me and Brian. When Sonny and Tessa were babies, we often talked about how one day, we would show them the world. Explore places that others only read about in books. Climb ruins in Athens, wander through bamboo forests in Japan, use chopsticks in Vietnam. 'We'll do it someday', we promised as we kissed each other goodnight and turned out the light.

But as the years passed, those conversations grew less and less frequent, and gradually, the dream died. Fizzled out by the reality of heavy mortgages, formal education, and businesses that required both partners to babysit for eleven months and twenty days of the year.

But that night at the campsite was different.

Our old conversation was back. Born again. Pulled up from under the weeds. Raised out of the ashes. And rather than see blockages and obstacles and no's, we saw only possibilities and potentials and why-the-hell-nots.

I will never forget how I felt that night.

It was magical. Uplifting. Exciting. The wine and words never ceased to flow. I remember looking up at the cloudless navy sky and wishing I could bottle the positivity. Keep it forever.

The next morning, I expected to get up and find the itch gone. To feel embarrassed and a bit sore. We've all been there, haven't we? When what seems like the best idea ever at half past eleven at night suddenly seems ridiculous and absurd at ten past nine in the morning. Nights like that are usually followed by mornings where you say, 'We really need to cut down on how much we drink. I think we're alkies. Let's only drink wine at the weekend from now on'.

But that wasn't one of those mornings.

Instead of being brought to our senses by the sunshine, we were more eager and determined.

The itch was still there. Bigger and ticklier than before.

And yes. It's true; we were slightly hungover. But who cares? We were on holiday. Anyway, everyone knows that red wine is good for unblocking the arteries. Ask the Greeks, they'll tell you. Why else do you think their country is in the Blue Zone?

For the remainder of our camping trip, we talked of nothing else. The dream reawakened. The plan began to hatch. We put our heads together like a couple of lovebirds and thought long and hard about the possibility of doing the thing we would remember forever … leaving everything behind and taking a year out of our lives to travel the world with our kids.

I hate it when holidays come to an end. It's rubbish.

Brushed and left out to dry (*do I have the only husband in history that does this with the tent before he packs it away?*), the groundsheet and tent were folded and packed into their respective bags. Returned to the top shelf of the shed shelf for another year. Brian reluctantly went back to his business, and I continued homeschooling the kids. Or at least tried to. For the most part, I spent hours daydreaming about what our twelve-month adventure could look like. Playing out scenarios in my head.

I knew it was possible.

We'd been homeschooling for six years, and the kids had made excellent academic progress (*it'd almost killed me, but that's another story for another time*). Sonny was way ahead of his peers. At sixteen, he had already gained every qualification he needed to apply for university. Most of his work was online. He could easily go.

Tessa was thirteen—a middle schooler. She was yet to start her formal exams and was at an age where a year travelling the world would benefit her far more than any textbook. I would get excited at the thought of her discovering new cultures, trying new foods, and speaking different languages.

Then I'd panic and tell myself she'd probably hate it. But that was okay because we'd take the iPad. If she got bored, she could always watch *Stranger Things*. There's a lot to be said for gaining knowledge from a bunch of screwed-up juvenile vampires.

In the months that followed, Brian and I talked of nothing else. We wrote down lists of pros and cons and asked ourselves if we had what it took to throw everything into the air and bugger off for a year.

Desire? Tick.

Kids? Tick.

Dog? Tick (My mum had kindly offered to have her for a year. Phew.)

Money? Wunh-wunh.

Almost enough money? Wunh-wunh.

Maybe some savings-hidden-under-the-bed money? Wunh-wunh.

Shit.

We sat down and did some sums. Juggled numbers. Offered suggestions.

'We could rent out the house while we are away', I said, sucking the end of my pen and then tapping it against my front teeth in an attempt to look intelligent and thoughtful. 'The money we'd make would easily cover the mortgage, and the rest would pay for the flights'.

Agreed. Next?

'And we could sell your half of the business. Take the money and use it for our trip?'

Not so sure…

Chins were rubbed. What we were suggesting was a big risk. That money was supposed to be for our golden years. Put aside to pay for a double room in the local retirement village.

'Oh, let's just spend it!' I cried haphazardly, startling the dog and almost causing her to swallow her stone. 'When we get old, we can go and live with Sonny. We'll take his girlfriend, the one we locked in the bedroom for sixty years. She can clean our pissy sheets and floss your dentures'.

Brian was convinced. The business went up for sale.

Everyone was on board. The kids sold their favourite toys to raise money, and I spent hours typing into Google: "How to travel the world cheaply".

While researching, I discovered a concept called "Couchsurfing", where you stay on people's couches around the world for free. (When they visit your country, you return the favour.) I figured if we coupled that with very cheap accommodations and only ever ate really cheap street food (and maybe a few worms), we could manage on next to nothing.

We set our budget at one hundred New Zealand dollars a day. For the four of us.

Perfect.

We didn't tell the kids about the budget. Not straight away. My motherly instincts told me to wait until they were trapped on the plane with no way out. Break the news to them then. No child wants to hear they'll be dossing on strangers' couches and living off egg noodles for a year of their life. Not when they've just parted with their favourite *Harry Potter* figures.

Everything was falling into place—like it was meant to be.

Not that it was all plain sailing. It wasn't. There were days when I would get cold feet. Nights when I'd wake up at 3 a.m. with my heart racing, drenched in sweat and panic. Thinking of all the things that could possibly go wrong. I'd lay there and ask myself *what the hell are you doing? This is mental! You will fail!*

But when those days came along, I tried to give myself grace (or a punch in the face depending on my hormones) and remind myself that I didn't have to make this trip perfect.

I just had to make it happen.

'If you don't go, then you'll never know!' My mum sang cheerfully down the phone. 'What's the worst that can happen? If you run out of money, you come home. If you argue with Brian, say sorry. And if the kids don't get along ... well ... well ...'

'Then I'll bash their heads together and leave them to rot at the side of the road in India'.

Silence.

'Sorry, Mum. Not really. Just joking. Mum? Mum? Hello? That was a joke…You'll still have the dog, won't you, Mum?'

The months rolled around, and before we knew it, we'd sold the business, readied the house for renters, and set a date to leave. The kids had even agreed to the four of us sharing a room.

'As long as it's not every night', Tessa said uneasily. She looked to Brian and then back to me. 'It's just that you breathe really loudly through your mouth, and it makes the room smell'.

Insolent child.

She'd regret those words when I was dead.

What thirteen-year-old wouldn't want to share a room with her parents? Even if the mother does suffer from occasional bouts of obstructive sleep apnoea and eats lots of garlic.

In the weeks leading up to our departure, we sat around the table discussing the thrilling things that lay ahead.

'I want to go to Japan and see a real samurai', said Sonny.

'I can't wait to go to London and shop in Harrods!' Tessa added.

'I'm just looking forward to being together as a family every day for a whole year', beamed Brian. (*Effing goody-goody. Why does he always have to be the one who manages to say the right thing?*)

My turn.

'I long for the day when I wake up and feel as free as a bird! Like those backpackers we met at Kerosene Creek. Tweet, tweet, whoopee!'

Awkward. Si. Lence.

Sonny narrowed his eyes and looked slightly repulsed as he recalled the memory. 'What? The ones with the black hairy armpits and the stinky towels?'

'Yes!' I replied giddily, slapping my knees and causing them to wobble like two big pink blancmanges. 'Those ones!'

I was excited.

This trip would be the making of me. For too many years, I'd hidden my light under a bushel. Been a wife and a mum and behaved the way society expected a middle-aged woman to behave. Enough was enough. It was time to show the kids what a cool, hip mum they really had.

I looked at my family and smiled with my teeth. They exchanged nervous glances.

Like a butterfly breaking free from its mothy, cystitis-y shell, I was ready.

Ready to fly.

Chapter Three
New York

Have you ever watched a film set in a really glamourous city, and no sooner do the credits roll up, you're on the internet, booking flights and making plans to experience the place yourself? But then when you arrive, it's crap, and you're like, *huh? This isn't how it's supposed to be. I want my money back.*

That was me. The film was *Big,* and the city was New York. But my experience wasn't worse than the film. Or even the same. It was better.

Far better.

New York City is the only place in the world you can visit at Christmas and not feel as though everything the movies have fed you is a big fat lie. It's all there: The snow, the ice rinks, the yellow cabs with the honking horns. Steaming fire hydrants, soaring skyscrapers, twinkling fairy lights strung from broad trees. Bustling elegant shops and glitzy restaurants with door attendants in top hats.

I even saw a flying elf in red boots drinking eggnog.

Starting the trip in New York had always been part of my master plan. Mainly because I needed some bartering power; it's far easier to convince your children to go backpacking around Asia and sleep on strangers' couches when you have a carrot to dangle. And for me, that carrot was New York. At Christmas.

I made sure to lay the foundations early. Six months before leaving for our trip.

'Can you believe it?' I'd gushed. 'You're going to New York City! You'll get to stay in a skyscraper taller than the clouds! You can go Christmas shopping and play in Central Park with Macaulay Culkin; it's going to be AMAZING!'

My plan worked perfectly. It was December, and here we were, a few weeks into our world trip, having just left JFK airport. On a bus heading to our hotel. In New York.

The kids were buzzing, hopping with excitement—their phones flying in every direction as they snapped photos of buildings and people and taxis, all to send back to their sad little friends, with their boring little lives in rubbish New Zealand.

'OMG! Look, Sonny!' Tessa squealed in delight. 'There's Manhattan! Where the big Coca-Cola sign is and the bridge that

Giselle walked along in *Enchanted*! If we stay on this side of the bus, we'll see the Empire State Building!' She pulled her brother by the arm, and they pressed their foreheads to the steamy window, craning their necks in the direction of the lights.

I looked at my children and smiled. Such darlings.

And then the bus turned left.

I'd booked us into a hotel in Queens. In one of the less affluent areas. It was one of those two-star jobbies that snobs on Trip Advisor refer to as doss-holes, but savvy budgeters like me call no-frills-and-not-bad-for-the-price bargains.

I'd always wanted to tell people we were staying in Queens. It doesn't get cooler than that. John Travolta lived in Queens. He worked in the local hardware store and danced with Annette every Friday night. And now there we were. Living the dream. Eating the big apple.

The bus stopped, and we climbed off, swinging our heavy backpacks onto the pavement.

When we planned for this trip, we'd intended to pack light. Take only three pairs of undies, some pants and maybe a couple of cotton tee-shirts. What we'd forgotten was that we would be visiting America first. In the depths of winter. And unless we wanted to freeze to death, we'd need warm clothes. So, along came the thick fleecy trousers and "my favourite hot water bottle." (No lie.) It's a wonder the airlines didn't make us pay for an extra seat with the amount of excess weight we'd brought with us.

The entrance to our hotel was on the opposite side of the street. As promised, I made sure we were staying in a skyscraper. Admittedly, it wasn't the sort of skyscraper the kids were expecting. Still, the hotel was on top of a gym, a swimming pool, a wine warehouse, a launderette, a twenty-four-hour Indian supermarket, and a car park with an uppy-downy barrier. In my eyes, that counted as a skyscraper.

'Where's Broadway?' asked Tessa, staring in disbelief at the higgledy-piggledy monstrosity.

There was an icy silence. The bus drove away, leaving us standing in a cloud of fumes.

New York in December is cold—freezing cold.

The salty sidewalks are thick with people, each doing their best to keep warm and reach their destination without losing a toe to frostbite.

It's easy to spot a local New Yorker; they dress in thin, warm layers. They wear woollen pea coats with folded cashmere scarves or duck-down jackets with Elmer Fudd-style hats.

I'd love to be a New Yorker.

They're hip and sophisticated—even when they wear a hat that makes them look like a Basset Hound dog.

I read somewhere that if you want to look like a native New Yorker in winter, you must dress in dark colours. 'Only lady Gaga fans and embarrassing tourists wear bright colours', warned the article's writer, 'and nobody wants to look like either of those'.

No way. Not me. Heaven forbid.

Today was the day the kids had been waiting for. We were going Christmas shopping in New York. I had decided to wear my yellow coat—the garishly luminous one.

'Wouldn't you be more comfortable in Sonny's brown fleece?' Tessa asked. Her eyes narrowed in disapproval. We stood in the cold, waiting for the train bound for Manhattan, 'I'm just thinking of you'.

I yanked up the zip, making sure to lift my chin out of the way.

'No need!' I said gleefully. 'This coat is just the ticket'.

And it was.

I'd bought my bright yellow coat two months earlier from a second-hand clothing website in New Zealand, especially for this trip. I remember the day it arrived through the post. I was well-chuffed. 'What a bargain!' I'd bragged. 'Thirty dollars for a fully waterproof coat with an inside pocket and a hood!'

'It's a bit … florescent', Brian had said as he watched me try it on. 'It reminds me of something a construction worker would wear'.

'Rubbish!' I replied, twirling around in front of the mirror, like Big Bird from *Sesame Street*. 'You're just jealous because your North Face coat doesn't have a flappy bit behind the collar'.

The train from Queens to Manhattan filled up quickly. Brian and I sat across from our young teenagers, witnessing their excitement as they counted off the stops to Times Square.

Silly children.

With just three days in New York, I had no intention of wasting time swanning around expensive shops and pretending to have money. No, thank you. Not on our budget. I had other plans.

'Wait', said Sonny as we disembarked the train six stops early at Canal Street. 'I thought you said we were going Christmas shopping today?'

We stepped onto the dimly lit platform and huddled together. The train pulled away, blasting the station with an arctic wind. Tessa's teeth chattered. 'That's right', I said, searching the overhead signs for the correct exit. 'I did. And that's exactly what we're going to do'.

'So why didn't we take the train to Times Square? Like the woman at the hotel told us to do?'

I took a breath. A fresh crowd of people had entered the platform. The noise level rose. My coat was too tight, and my head was beginning to itch. I wanted to kill my son, and it was only ten past eleven in the morning. The mithering persisted.

'I don't get it', he bleated. 'Why are we here? How far is the Rockefeller Center? When are we going to that famous street that Casey Neistat lives on? I told Josh I'd get a photo of it. And don't forget I can't walk far. My socks are rubbing, and I've got blisters'.

Eff me. All those words, taken in a single breath.

For a brief second, I imagined what would happen if I booted my son across the platform.

Just a little kick…

I blinked and rubbed my hands together like Bob Cratchit. Ashamed of my weirdness. This was New York! This was going to be fun!

'Come on', I said, deciding to make more of an effort to like my children and be normal. 'Let's get out of here. And don't you worry; you'll like where we're going. Just you wait and see!'

The four of us made our way towards the stairs, jostling ahead with a small army of people. A young couple descended the stairs opposite us, walking in sync, arms wrapped around each other's waists. Smiling. Refusing to be parted.

I looked at Brian. Leading the way with his neck jutted forwards and his lips set tight. He was on a mission. Subways were dangerous places. I touched his elbow and attempted to start a conversation. Hoping to loosen him up and unhinge his jaw.

'I wonder why ceramic tiles are always used in subway stations?' I asked girlishly.

His shoulders broadened. *Bingo.* I knew that'd do the trick. 'Well', he began, his pace unaltered, 'City dwellers in the Victorian era valued cleanliness and hygiene. So much so that they would—'

Boring bastard.

I switched places with Tessa.

It's always a bit of a shock when you emerge from a subway station and enter the real world. The light hurts your eyes, and the traffic noise offends. It takes a moment to adjust.

We stood on the pavement next to a street vendor selling rechargeable batteries and Adidas trainers. A cluster of sightseers congregated next to us. Someone had obviously told them that the entrance to a busy train station was an excellent place to open a huge gigantic map.

Sonny scanned the street and scowled. 'I don't see Macy's', he mumbled sarcastically.

One, two, three …. Let it go, Liz.

I breathed in the cold air and began to hum the song that Elsa sang in *Frozen.*

'Mm, mm, mmmm, du, du duuuuu…'

Tessa looked from her brother and back to me nervously. 'Don't, Sonny ...' she said under her breath. 'Just leave it'.

'It's all right for you, Tessa …. You don't have a friend who wanted you to get a photo, and a—'

I let out a long heavy nose breath and closed my eyes. The chittering stopped. The map folded. The man on the stall shuffled closer and re-arranged his batteries.

'If you must know', I said, inflating my chest and doubling the circumference of my breasts, 'we're going to the Chinatown shops. Where the *real* stuff is. The cheap deals. You might not realise this, but WE are on a budget, and I didn't come to NYC to be taken for a MUG'.

I turned on my heel and stormed away, leaving my sixteen-year-old son glued to the spot. His cheeks red with shame from being scolded on the streets of New York by his mother. Next to a man selling trainers.

'Can you please stop calling it NYC?' he called after me defiantly. 'It's sooo extra'.

Lower Manhattan Chinatown is wonderful. Like an Asian version of Bogner Regis, only smellier and without the sand.

Multicoloured shops entice passers-by with ten-dollar massages and plastic shoes shaped like crocodiles. Wooden wind chimes, mobile phones, and pink hoodies embossed with "I Love NYC" clog the pavements and food markets with live frogs and dead ducks live alongside obscure-looking vegetables resembling something that Dr Seuss invented.

We stood at the end of Mott Street, Chinatown's main drag, breathing in the scene.

'We will buy our Christmas gifts from here', I announced like Gandalf.

Tessa's jaw dropped. She'd waited eleven months for this day— eleven months to tell her friends that she was Christmas shopping in America. In New York. New York City. Now, here she was, faced with nothing but incense sticks, calligraphy sets, and those weird brass bells that are said to bring Chinese people luck.

We were hungry, so we agreed to eat lunch before shopping.

'I saw a Benny and Jerry's by the metro', Sonny offered. He waved his phone in the air, desperately searching for a sliver of signal to reveal the ice cream location and take him far, far away from the smell of star anise.

'God, no', I said, shaking my head disapprovingly like an old granny who'd just discovered the milkman was sleeping with someone called Ernie. 'Not American food. Let me ... think .... How about we buy something from a market? Yes, let's do that! We'll get a picnic lunch and eat it on the go'.

(*I find one-sided conversations are the only way forward when making a family decision.)

The kids hate it when I use the words "on the go". They know it's code for sharing. The brief flash of excitement over the suggestion of lunch evaporated instantly.

I knew exactly where to go.

At the far end of Mott Street was a large indoor food market selling every Chinese food item imaginable. A squishy floor made from black rubber tiles led to an open front facing the road. Outside on the pavement were a number of plastic buckets which held mostly chicken beaks and other gross animal parts. Every few minutes, a staff member wearing knee-high white rubber boots and a pair of overalls came to the front of the store with a hose and washed down the blood and guts from the floor.

I'd read about this place when researching where to buy cheap Chinese food in Chinatown several months earlier, and now here we were, standing right outside.

'Here it is!' I trilled, nodding and smiling at my own researching brilliance. 'We'll buy our lunch from here'.

We stood on the road opposite and took in the sprawling emporium before us.

Tessa turned a shade of green. She swallowed hard. 'Oh no. Please … not here …. The smell gives me anxiety. Remember that time I was really sick at Terry Thomson's KFC party, and his aunty, who used to work at the drive-through, said it was because the place was rank and the owners used chicken feet instead of proper meat?' She stopped to catch her breath. 'Please … please, can we go somewhere else …?'

She looked to Brian for support. He took her hand and squeezed it reassuringly. 'It's okay, Tess. There'll be something you like. Don't worry. I bet there's pasta or crisps or something'.

Tessa snuggled into Brian's arm and looked up at him as if to say, 'I love you so much, Daddy. I wish it was just you and me on this trip'. And then Brian looked at me and smiled as if to say, 'She'll always be our baby'.

Blah, blah, blah. Unadventurous idiots.

I marched across the road like a giant daffodil, leaving the rest of the family to follow. Two cars came from either direction, and one of them stopped. The driver waved us across. *How nice.* I shrugged my shoulders playfully and shouted into his windscreen, using my best New York accent, 'Fuhgeddaboudit, I'm warkin' here!'

The man looked alarmed. Brian offered an apologetic wave, and Sonny muttered, 'I can't believe this is happening to me'.

Leaving my limpet children and their sympathetic father outside, I trotted into the marketplace alone. I was hungry, and the smell of food was reeling me in like a river trout.

The place buzzed with energy. Noise, colours, smells, and hundreds of people pushing and shoving, waving their money in the air to jump the line. Co-workers hollered across the room to each other, communicating in a fast and incompressible language.

Rows of glass counters displayed exotic food: pigs' knuckles, live rock cod, dried shrimp, alligator meat. Piles of freshly cooked dumplings sandwiched alongside plates laden with dim sum and noodles, slathered in sticky sauces. Shredded pig's ear, gamey beef tongue and fried rice. There were even dedicated sweet displays with pyramids of perfectly baked egg tarts.

I felt like Augustus Gloop in the chocolate river.

I watched as the man beside me confidently ordered a whole lacquered roasted duck smothered in a dark plum sauce. He paid and was handed his goods in a clear plastic container.

Excellent. Just what I was looking for. A nice ducky picnic. That'd go down a treat with my loved ones.

I peered through the glass cabinet in search of the biggest bird.

'Erm ... could I please have a—'

'No English', snapped the old woman behind the counter. Her wrinkled lips had been carelessly lined with a pink pencil, and she wore a faded flowery tabard. She wagged a finger disapprovingly and raised her thin eyebrows impatiently. 'Huh?'

Old bag. How rude.

I blushed and pointed to the fattest duck at the front of the counter. She ignored me and lifted out the one next to it—the skinny one.

'Twelve dollars fifty', she said in a perfectly clipped Oxford accent. 'Next person in line, please'.

I returned to my family. We stood outside. Trying to decide on a suitable place to eat.

'I can't eat standing up, Liz', Brian complained. 'Not with the way my hips are. I'll check on Google Maps and see if there's a park close by'. He took out his phone. Tessa rubbed his back dotingly and smiled as if to say, 'Don't worry, Daddy, when she dies, I'll look after you'.

The temperature of the duck's body in the plastic container was cooling quickly. I swallowed. *Google Maps, my arse.* My eyes searched the street hungrily. *Yes!* Across from the food shop, stacked up at the side of the road, was a pile of wooden pallets. 'There!' I said, pointing to my find. 'We'll sit on those!'

Ignoring the moans and the protests about how it was "dangerous" and "probably illegal", I climbed up onto the tower and took my place. The kids refused to join me; they said they'd rather stand.

'How about you Bri? Up you come'. I shuffled an inch to the left and tapped the wood to show him there was room. Tessa shivered. Brian took off his scarf and wrapped it around her neck, then hooked the top of his coat up over his chin.

'No … you're alright, Liz … I'll wait down here. I don't want to risk snagging my new nylon pants'.

Wet willy wuss.

'Fine', I said. 'Have it your way. I'll sit up here alone'. I extended my neck and pretended to admire the view. Like a ginormous canary on a perch.

Making myself as comfortable as I could on the pile of packing crates, I carefully opened the lid of the plastic container. A waft of steam moistened my face, and the smell of softly spiced cardamon and cloves filled my nostrils.

Yum.

Drool seeped from the corners of my mouth. I licked my lips.

'I thought you told us that when you came to New York on your honeymoon, you ate bagels and cream cheese in a café overlooking a church?' said Sonny, kicking the bottom pallet sulkily and causing my make-shift restaurant to wobble precariously. 'Why do we have to stand in the street and eat boiled duck served from an ice cream container?'

I wanted to tell him there were lots of things we used to do before he came along, but I remained silent. Now wasn't the time for a sex education lesson.

Not when Brian was wearing those clingy nylon pants.

I wiggled my fingers over the meat in giddy anticipation. 'Who minds if I go first?' I sang, tilting my head to the side in an attempt to look cute. Brian cleared his throat and looked away. He didn't like it when I used my baby voice in public. It frightened him.

Sonny folded his arms and arched his back. 'Go for it', he said. 'It's not like we're desperate or anything'.

I pulled a hunk of oily flesh from the bird's leg and dunked it in the pool of sweet sauce, ramming it into my open mouth together with a piece of crispy skin. 'Mmmmm …' I chomped down hard to extract every bit of flavour.

My God, it was divine. The best thing ever.

'Deeee-licious!' I spluttered, speckling my yellow coat in orange spit.

Brian looked repulsed. He buried his nose deeper into his coat and rubbed his chin against the inner fleece lining.

A woman in a Gucci trench coat came striding along the pavement towards us. She scanned our family and flashed us a look of curiosity mixed with pity. Her hand went to her purse. I smiled and offered a friendly little wave. She crossed the road.

Tessa pressed her thumb into the palm of her hand and stared at her feet.

'Who wants some?' I said, lowering the container to a height nobody could reach.

Both kids dipped their fingers in the sauce but refused anything else, and Brian picked at the meat like an anorexic sparrow. I had the meal to myself. *Lucky me!* Ten minutes later, the duck carcass sat naked, every shred of meat devoured.

I stood on the pavement and wiped the oily grease from my lips. I rubbed my swollen stomach and let out a sneaky sideways burp to give myself a little breathing space. Brian turned away.

'Righteo', I said enthusiastically, 'who's ready to hit those Christmas gifts?'

Our eyes fell to the shop across the road. The one selling paper lanterns and nodding white ceramic cats.

'If I started walking right now', asked Sonny, 'how long do you think it would take me to get to Broadway?'

CHAPTER FOUR
SRI LANKA

Nor Julia Roberts

always panicking

Impatient Prat

I'm not one to moan. It's not in my nature. I strive to remain positive at all times.

I take copious amounts of hormone therapy and consume lots of wine to aid this, but sometimes, even that's not enough, and the odd whinge manages to blast its way out of my mouth and eyeballs.

The truth is I thought that travelling the world would be lovely and romantic and perfect. But it isn't. Not always. Sometimes it's hideous and smelly. And disastrous. To illustrate this (and so you won't think I'm an exaggerating lightweight), I have decided to share a story. Something that happened at a train station in Sri Lanka.

Then you'll believe me. Then you'll see.

I wasn't going to tell you this. I said, *no, Liz. That's disgusting. Don't. That's not the sort of thing you should include in your book. What if the kids read it?*

But to be honest, I'm past caring. I couldn't give a toss. I'm desperate. Someone's going to hear about it, and that someone is going to be you. And anyway, who am I kidding? As if either of my kids will read this book. Fat chance. Far too many words.

So here it is. The tale of the harem pants and what happened to them in Sri Lanka.

*Apologies to my kids in advance. Just in case. You never know; Elon might invent a rocket that blasts your iPhones to the moon, leaving you with nothing but eye contact and paperback books.

Sri Lanka, the pearl of the Indian Ocean. A country of gentle people, lush tropical landscape and heavenly warm waters.

The air in Sri Lanka is humid and laden with comforting smells. Turmeric, cinnamon, and the waft of burning leaves from the small street fires mingle to create a fragrance that can only be described as … Sri Lankan. Wild Jasmine grows in the hedges, beautifully fragrant and sweet, enticing even the most hard-core coffee addicts to switch to tea.

Then there's Sri Lanka at night. Magical. The starlit lanes filled with the banter of frogs that chorus from the paddy fields. The tiny fireflies that light the way with their fairy-tale sparkles. It's gorgeous.

But.

Not every experience in Sri Lanka is pleasant. Take pissing your pants and being forced to sit in them for hours on a train, for instance.

That's not marvellous. No nice jasmine flowers and froggy spawn then.

There's something about the smell of dried urine. It has a habit of … lingering.

The train journey from Marissa to Colombo is one of the most beautiful rides in the world. It is quite breath-taking. If you do it, I recommend you splash out and take one of the fast trains instead of the slower ones. Tickets cost only a dollar more, but the difference in trains is huge. One is quite comfortable and (semi) normal, while the other is clapped out, knackered, and full-on shit.

We took the cheaper option. Obviously. Those dollars add up when you multiply them by four.

'Why do we have to go on the slowest train?' whined the kids the night before when I told them the usual two-hour journey would take four.

We were sitting at a small open-air restaurant on the side of the road, eating egg curry from plastic plates. I pondered the question. Tilted my head to the side so I'd look cultured and brainy like one of those students who go on *University Challenge* and press the buzzer before the host has finished talking.

Hmm.

If I was an uncaring mother who wanted nothing more than to destroy her children's self-esteem with my wicked words, I might have said, 'Because it's cheaper and being on the train for four hours means I don't have to buy you lunch. Plus, I'm tired. And I hate you'.

But I'm not, and I don't. So I didn't.

I popped the last bit of flaky roti into my mouth and pressed my fingers hard onto the plate to collect the remaining crumbs. I swallowed. 'So you'll get to see more of the country'. I beamed, cheerfully. 'And with four hours to spare, you'll have lots of time to draw pretty pictures and make notes for your next project. Hurray for homeschooling!'

Sonny scowled. Tessa slumped. Brian asked for the bill.

The day didn't get off to a good start.

I had decided to wear my hippy harem pants for the train journey of a lifetime. The ones with the meter-wide elasticated waist that pulls up nice and high under my boobs and conceals my rollies. I had been saving them, especially for Asia. And now, here they were. Ready to make their debut.

I stood in front of the oblong mirror glued to the wall of the shared room and turned from side to side to admire my reflection. Tessa sat on the bed behind me, her knees pulled up under her chin.

Frowning.

There was a time, back in the olden days, when anything I did, wore, or said to my daughter was received with open arms. She would spend hours drawing pictures of the two of us. Childish stick figures, etched in crayon, wearing triangular skirts and holding hands. Outlined in a love heart with the words "Mummy and Tessa" written above it.

Up until about five years ago, I could have put a dustbin bag on my head, and Tessa would have clasped her hands in glee and told me I looked like Cinderella.

But those days were gone.

'Oh, Mummy …' she said, staring at my tent-like balloon legs incredulously. 'Why are you wearing *those*?'

My left eyelid spasmed.

She wrapped her arms around her legs protectively and went on. 'They're stretched and filthy and …' I waited. She took a deep breath. 'And BIG'.

Thoughtless madam. She'd have rollies one day.

I ruffled the front of my hair, adjusting strands to cover the deep frown lines etched between my eyebrows.

It was on the tip of my tongue to say: 'Because, my darling, I look like a hippy goddess in these pants. Meaning everyone around me will think I've come from a meditation retreat in Tibet and that you two aren't my real children but some helpless bratty orphanage kids I'm taking on my spiritual pilgrimage. To cleanse your soul and teach you how to spell'.

But I didn't.

No child wants to be labelled dyslexic. Not when they've been homeschooled by their mother and have no proper qualifications.

'Shut up, and don't pass personal remarks', I quipped. Then I straightened my knickers and smiled into the mirror, secretly congratulating myself for practising Asian mindfulness. *Well done, me.* Sri Lanka was having a positive impact on my parenting skills, it seemed.

One tuk-tuk ride and a horrendously hot walk later, the four of us huffed and puffed onto the railway station.

'Right', I said, throwing my pack onto the floor and wiping the sweat from my upper lip. 'First things first. Can anyone see a sign for the toilet? I'm dying'. I narrowed my eyes and scanned the platform. Hoping that I looked like sexy Stacy Sheridan from *T J Hooker* when she had a serious case to crack. 'Best to spend a penny here than on the train …. That's if there *are* any toilets on the train. What do you think, Brian? Is the bladder capable of holding on for four hours? Do you know if anyone has ever actually stopped the train to …' I turned around.

'Brian?'

The three of them had walked away. They were sitting on a bench further up the platform, laughing and comparing the size of their thumbs.

Humph. I folded my arms in a huff.

I'm not sure what has happened to me. Since starting this year-long trip, I've become obsessed with toilets. Fixated. I spend most of my waking days thinking about what the next toilet will be like, or worse still, telling anyone who'll listen about a recent lavvy experience that left its mark on me (excuse the pun). I can't stand it. If I'm not talking about my fibre intake (or lack of it), I'm quizzing the kids on their movements. The other night, I even dreamt I owned a toilet roll shop and that a load of birds (that weren't actually birds but rats with wings), broke in and stole my entire stock.

Poor Brian.

Not only does he have to watch as I sniff my clothes before wearing them, he now has to suffer regular updates on my bowel movements. 'Hard or soft? Yellow or brown? And, oh my god, what the hell is that piece of cord-looking-sinewy-stuff laced through my poo. Is that normal? Do you think I have a tumour?'

The other day I caught him looking at me.

Not in an alluring, wow-you're-the-mother-of-my-children-and-the-sexiest-woman-I've-ever-had-the-honour-of-travelling-the-world-with kind of way, but in the way you might look at an old woman with no teeth. Sitting at a bus stop sucking her thumb. Loudly.

Just think about that for a moment.

There you go. That's how he looked at me. Imagine that.

If you do decide to take the train from Mirissa to Columbo and find yourself at Weligama station, busting for the bog, be warned. While the toilets may look pretty from the outside, with pots of geraniums lining the doorway and signs written in golden letters, they are squat toilets.

Clean, squat toilets, admittedly, but *still* squat toilets.

If you're unfamiliar with this concept, let me explain how a squat toilet works. Unless you are wearing a skirt that you can hoik up around your waist or trousers you can somehow manage to take off (which, when you're standing in a four-by-four cubicle with nothing but three walls, a door and a hole in the ground is neigh on impossible), you will struggle.

Not only must you aim your goings-on into the hole, but you must also make sure that the lower half of your clothing remains dry.

Free from flow.

Which, when you are an idiot like me who has chosen to wear stupidly baggy pants with masses of material, is not easy.

I lowered myself down and positioned myself over the long-drop. Squatted. Ready to do my business. Thighs shaking. Mouth rammed with as much trouser material as I could manage without gagging.

'Ahhhh …yeeessssss'.

I emptied my bladder and peered between my legs. (*I'm not quite sure why women do this when we're squatting, but we do. Always.*) Down into the urine-stained hole. Only to see the crutch of my baggy pants dragging in the rush of pee. Swirling around. The thin material soaking up the yellow liquid like a sponge.

Shit. Piss. Fanny. I stood up. Sweating. Holding onto the sides of the walls for support. *Great. Now, what am I supposed to do?* There are no posh hand blowing machines in Sri Lanka to dry my dripping pants. No tissues to mop up the moisture.

Shit.

'Ding-doong. Foreign-talk-foreign-talk-foreign-talk-COLOMBO-foreign-talk-foreign-talk. Ding-dong'.

Bugger.

Fuck.

I pulled up my wet pants. Gathering, squeezing and wringing while at the same time pushing open the door with my foot. I took a breath: *dignity and composure, Liz. Hold your head high. Even the Queen does wees and poos.*

I turned left and walked along the platform. Down the runway of shame. My warm wet thighs rubbing together. My smelly baggy pants flapping from side to side.

Chaffing me with every step.

The baggy pants I'd worn because, secretly, I'd believed I would look like Julia Roberts in *Eat, Pray, Love.*

My cheeks glowed like a furnace as I walked towards Brian with the giant soiled, sodden nappy—swinging between my legs. *Almost there, Liz. Keep your cool. Remember. Some men get turned on by urine.*

'Where've you been?'

Brian frowned and tutted, then tapped his watch impatiently. He showed no sign of arousal.

I flicked my hands out in front of me, pretending that I'd just washed them. 'That's me, all done. Nose powdered and ready to go!' Then I turned towards the tracks and looked into the distance pensively.

Like Julia Roberts. In *Squat, Piss, Spray.*

When you travel third-class on a train in Sri Lanka, you sit where you can. There are no seat numbers or allocated places; it's each man for their own. We boarded and scattered in different directions.

'Is this seat taken?' I said to a blonde woman who sat balancing a baby on her lap.

The infant gurgled. The woman sniffed and frowned.

'Please', she said politely, gesturing to the place next to her. She shuffled closer to the window. I smiled and sat down in my own little puddle of pongy piss.

Ahhh. That's better.

Seats on Sri Lankan trains are sectioned into groups of four. Two going backwards, two facing forwards. A young couple sat in the seat opposite. A man and a woman. Sharing a book. I smiled and cleared my throat as if to say, 'Who fancies a chat?' but they ignored me. The girl's eyes moved from side to side. She twitched her nose and turned a page.

Hmm. Not very polite. Probably from North Dakota or Greenland or somewhere. I remember reading that people in those faraway places have a bit of an attitude.

I shifted closer to the child. Savouring the smell of baby powder and milky skin.

'Hello, cutieee', I said, nodding my head agreeably so the mother didn't think I was a child trafficker. 'How old are youuuu?'

'Goo-goo-ga-ga'.

Stupid question, really. Given that the kid was a blob. Imagine if it had answered? It would've been whipped off the train and inducted into The World Book of Records as the most advanced human genius ever.

The woman smiled awkwardly. She brushed the child's soft hair to one side and touched its chin affectionately.

'She's four months'.

I laughed and widened my eyes.

'Four months? WOW!'

I have no idea why I laughed or why I said, 'Wow'. And from the look on her face, neither did the mother. She seemed puzzled. Was I insinuating that her child was an overfed pig? Or was my 'Wow' a way of saying that her baby was hideously small and thin, and had obviously not developed properly due to malnutrition?

I blinked and backtracked.

'She looks just like a four-month-old should look'.

'Yes … thank you. She does'.

The woman moved the baby from one knee to the other and pointed out of the window. Pretending to look at something that wasn't even there.

Snotty Cow. Some people are so sensitive.

I thought about confronting her. The woman. Giving her a piece of my mind. Pulling her perfectly plaited hair and shouting into her face: 'I'm not stupid! I know why you don't want me to hold your bubba. You can smell *the smell*'.

But I didn't. Because only crackpots do things like that. And the last thing I wanted was to be reported to the Thai station master for rowdy and unruly behaviour.

I took the tiger balm out of my flight bag—the one I keep for Brian's stiff back—and had a little sniff. Then I folded my hands in my lap and pouted, taking in the woman's pocketed shorts with my eyes. Starchy, light brown and knee length.

Very sensible.

I wanted to ask her if she was a desert park ranger, but it was clear she didn't want to talk. Shame really. We could have been the best of friends, me and her. Bonded. Mama to mama.

I could have told her about the white tendony thing living in my poo.

I'm not a fan of PDA (public displays of affection for those without teenagers and not in the know like me). I think it's a cheap way to show off and make others feel barren and haggard. 'Look how happy we are together! We have sex every night. Sometimes twice! We can't get enough of each other! He won't leave me alone! I even sleep naked!'

Shagger braggers. That's what I call them.

I peered at the girl opposite me. The one with the book and an appetite for her boyfriend's ear. She was young and beautiful. A lovely young travel girl. No more than twenty-five with chestnut-coloured hair pulled back from her pretty face by one of those floral headbands that twisted in a knot at the top.

I used to have a headband like that.

I stopped wearing it when Brian asked me the name of the actress that played Hilda Ogden in *Coronation Street*.

I took the Kindle from my bag and hid behind it. Pretending to read but secretly spying on the pair. Him, with his Jesus sandals and sun-bleached hair. Her, with her perfectly painted burgundy toenails, wearing one of those silver jewelled toe rings. Sprawled across him like a lazy cat. Taking up both seats. One smooth brown leg draped over his knee, the other tip-tapping suggestively against his calf like a flippity floozy.

I looked down at my fat little trotters. Swollen and bloated and retaining enough water to bathe an elephant.

No one tells you when you travel the world that not only will you have to carry a stupidly overpacked-and-ridiculously-heavy backpack wherever you go, but you will stand in line for everything. Airports. Visa offices. Ticket booths. Masses of people and never any chairs. Hours on end with your knees locked and the feeling in your feet fluctuating between numbness and pain.

I thought about warning the girl that crossing her legs would most certainly cause bulbous varicose veins in later years. But I remained silent and, instead, tapped my Kindle. Hoping that she'd see me and marvel at what a quick reader I was.

'Finished, honey?' The man kissed the top of her head tenderly.

'Not quite. Almost … there … three more lines … Done'.

The girl licked her finger and turned a page.

I slid my hand under my backside and sniffed my fingers discreetly. *Not too bad.*

Clickety-clack, clickety-clack, went the train.

What is that girl reading that is so damn interesting? What did the cover say? I couldn't see. Not without craning my head underneath her arm, and I didn't want to do that. Stinking of piss is one thing, but being labelled a whacko is quite another. I looked out the window.

'Gaga-goo-goo'.

The mother unbuttoned her shirt and lifted the child to her breast. Poor thing. I thought about offering my sympathy and telling her not to worry. Reassuring her that it wouldn't be long before the baby was gobbling a Big Mac and fries and that she wouldn't have to endure this form of cowism torture much longer. But she had her eyes closed and was humming. Pretending to like it. Probably trying to block out the pain of having an overfed giant with a huge brain biting at her tit.

I re-opened my Kindle and continued to perv at the shagger braggers.

The girl's head was now on the man's chest, her chin tilted upwards. Looking at him from upside down. Straight up his nostrils. She reached up playfully and took a strand of his hair, twisted it around her finger. Coiled it up and then let it bounce back down again.

'You're sooo cute, sugar pumpkin'. She giggled.

Blurggghhh. Gaaaagggg. Puke.

I crossed my legs and waited. Waited for him to explode and ram the book into her face. Tell her how annoying she was, and how her laying across him like that was giving him acidic reflux, and why couldn't she be more mature and sophisticated like that woman opposite? The one who smelled a bit putrid but looked like Julia Roberts.

But he didn't.

He looked down at her (because she was small and petite and he was a big tall, hunky giant) and mouthed, 'Hello ... you'.

Gasp! My eyes widened. The girl puckered her lips. He leaned over. She whimpered. *Oh my God ...*

SNAP!!

I closed my Kindle with force. The baby jolted. The nipple stretched. I shot an apologetic look at the mother. The couple looked alarmed. *What the??*

I crossed my arms to show my disapproval. To let the couple know that this had gone far enough. That it was time to put an end to this lewd and smutty behaviour.

Everyone held their breath.

If I was the sort of woman who was brave and didn't mind speaking out in public, like one of those people you hear about on The Tube in London, who stand up to muggers when they snatch their bag, I might have said, 'You two are gross. This has to stop! Get a room! There are women and children present. There's a place for shagger braggers like you, and this train ISN'T one of them'.

But I'm not, and they weren't, so I didn't.

Instead, I smiled prudishly and carefully positioned myself so that the yellow stain on my pants didn't show. Then I turned to the infant and said in my cutest mummy voice.

'Wad dat funny smell, bayyybbee?'

Chapter Five
India

It's funny now to think that India was the country I was most nervous about visiting. Yet, six weeks after arriving, when the time came to say goodbye, I couldn't bear to leave.

There are many things to love about India.

Magnetic. Mystical. Welcoming. Warm. India.

The lush green foliage that hangs over the dusty roads of Alappuzha. The narrow twisty lanes in Udaipur. The warmth and curiosity of the Indian people. The men with their constant talking and questioning. The women, with their flowing saris and multicoloured bangles that jingle as they wave their hands in the air to express themselves. The smell of warm chai flavoured with cinnamon and sugar. The sound of the morning prayers broadcast from tinny tannoys on the roofs. The beeping of horns, the ongoing and unfinished construction work, the raising of voices.

There's a constant hum in India. You can't get away from it. And for some strange reason, you never, ever want to.

But not everything is saris and sunshine in India. There were days when I would have gladly fizzled the fuzz and floated down the River Ganges in a twin tub…

I've always wanted to be flexible. Like those yoga bunnies that you see on Instagram. The ones with perky pecs and uppity boobs.

I've only ever been to one yoga class, and it scarred me for life. It was back in the nineties in England. I arranged for me and Brian to go to a "couples only" yoga session. I know. Don't. God knows what I was thinking. When I phoned to make the booking (this was before the internet and Calendly), I was told by Becks, the woman who ran the class, to bring an open mind and a double sleeping bag.

'Oh, and just to let you know, we can't take cheques, babes. Only cash, yeah?'

I knew the minute we arrived that we'd made a mistake. It was weird. A room filled with couples, all smiling and stretching together. Bending over each other. Connecting.

Awkward.

Brian and I hadn't been together that long, and back then, I wouldn't even let him put my dirty knickers in the washing machine (lucky for him, I have since relaxed my standards). I've never felt so self-conscious in all my life. Even my ears were blushing.

For the final ten minutes of the class, we were all told to lie down next to each other. In our shared sleeping bags. The other couples seemed to enjoy this. They were relaxed and at ease. Not me. I remember being annoyed because Brian's socks kept scratching against the inside of the blue nylon sleeping bag. The one we'd bought from Argos for nineteen quid.

I wanted to smash his face in.

We never went back. In fact, I never attended another yoga class ever again. Until now.

Because now I was in India. And everyone knows that yoga is better in India. It originated from there. That's right. Yoga was invented in India.

Five thousand years ago, while the rest of the world was running around in bearskins knocking things up out of bronze, a bloke named Shiva was out climbing a mountain. Getting some fresh air. When he got to the top peak, he decided to sit down. Take a breather. He crossed his legs and faced his palms upward. It felt good. After an hour or so, he realised that this was far better than being at home with the missus. Significantly less stressful. So he stayed there. For ages. And that's how yoga was born.

Honest.

We were in Gokarna, a small village in Karnataka on the Southwest coast of India.

Gokarna is gorgeous. Wonderfully quaint. It has pretty windy streets flanked by small colourful shops selling everything from intricately carved musical instruments to beautiful soft leather holdalls.

The people of Gokarna are friendly. Walk past any roadside stall, day or night, and the owner will, more often than not, offer up a smile and a wave. Greet you with the familiar 'Namaste'. *As a side note, the medicine kiosk on the corner sells Imodium if you are unfortunate enough to get the runs.*

Gokarna attracts a diverse mixture of characters. From the profoundly spiritual who explore ancient shrines and temples and wash their bodies in holy waters, to the yummy mummy yoga buffs who sit on the beach all day making ankle bracelets from their pubic hair.

If you come to Gokarna (which means cow's ear in Sanskrit), you must be the kind of person who is spiritually calm and horizontal.

You should practice world peace, never admit to having watched (and liked) *Miss World* on the telly, preferably be vegetarian, and you must never, ever raise your voice. Especially not in front of your kids.

The thing I love most about travelling is the unexpected encounters that lead to new discoveries.

Take me and yoga, for instance. Who'd have known that buried deep inside me was a churning desire to shed my restrictive clothing and bend my body on a rubber mat? Not me. I had no idea that entombed beneath the gooey intestines of my heart and soul was a little flower. A yoga bud. Longing to open and flourish and grow.

I thought I hated yoga. Detested it.

But no, apparently not. And if I hadn't come face to face with a certain woman in India, I might never have known.

Might never have opened that worm can and let my bud-ness sprout.

We were in a small cramped family restaurant at the end of the street in Gokarna, just about to order food, and in they walked. A mother, her husband and two small children. Floating into the room like four higher beings. Taking their seats at the table next to us.

I would have smiled and greeted them, but I was too busy trying to keep my hands from around Tessa's throat. Moments earlier, she had announced (again) that the only thing she would eat for dinner was chow mein.

As the perfect family took to their gentle seats, my angry inflated arse was rising from mine.

'Biryani, spinach and cheese curry, lentils, green pea soup, but no—all the way to India to eat "bloody Chinese"', I rattled off to my daughter, as she turned her nose up at every suggestion on the menu. 'No wonder you look so bloody thin and pale. Well, don't blame me when you're taken to an Indian hospital and fed through a drip'.

Nice Liz. Really nice.

The perfect family was reading the menu, seemingly uninterested in the family spat happening across from them. Their table surrounded by an air of confidence that can only be achieved by doing really cool stuff, such as trekking across a hot desert or wading through a muddy puddle in a jungle. Wearing nothing but a leather thong and a pendant containing Buddha's left eye.

I bet they're from the Netherlands. Or the Upper Midwest. They're all blonde and adventurous over there.

The perfect woman had two children. I wanted to holler across the table in an attempt to connect, 'You're just like us! We're the same!'

But I didn't.

I remained silent and gnawed at the skin around my thumbnail. I didn't want the perfect mother to think I had Tourette's.

The older child, who resembled Mowgli, was no more than eight. He wore a turban between his legs, and his hair looked as though it'd never seen conditioner in its life. The younger child, a baby, was pinned to its mother's chest. Held captive by one of those khaki green slings that hippies buy from festivals. His arms and legs spread eagle across the body of its beautiful mother.

You know how sometimes you can't help but stare? Well, that was me that night.

I gawped unashamedly. Drinking in every bit of the Earth Mother's beauty. From her sun-kissed arms adorned with layers of thin silver bangles to her perfectly white teeth. She was angelic. A calm and stretchy yoga goddess dressed in a yellow cheesecloth tee-shirt. Wearing no bra. Not even a strapless one. Laughing. Laughing with Mowgli. Talking to him. Listening, for real. Not even fake listening.

I watched in awe as she gathered handfuls of sun-bleached hair from behind her neck and pulled it across her shoulder, flashing a twinkly smile at her husband.

My eyes darted to him. The man. The father. Earth Mother's husband, smiling and unshaven. Wearing hessian pants he'd sewn together with camel hair. His chest was bare save for the string of orange beads that hung around his neck. The kind of beads that symbolise wisdom and goodness and make you a big strong man and a better person—a person who loves cows and henna and eats loads of quinoa without complaining that it tastes like chicken grit.

I looked across the table at Brian. He was wearing his black polyester tee-shirt. The shiny one. The one he got free from AliExpress when he spent $10 on brake fluid for the car.

I tried to imagine him bare-chested and wearing a set of nana beads. *Yuck.* A wave of nausea swept over me. I quickly obliterated the image. How silly of me. They would only stick to his chest hair when he started to sweat.

The perfect family ordered their food.

Mowgli chose the Dahl soup while the mother stroked his matted locks in approval. 'Yummy, isn't it, my darling?' she purred, with one skinny leg wrapped around the other.

I was suddenly reminded of those bendy pipe straws from primary school. The furry ones the teacher would fetch from the craft cupboard two weeks before Christmas and tell you to twist into the shape of a tree. But you could only ever manage to twist it into a cross. Which was quite handy, seeing as it was Christmas.

I looked across at Tessa, cagily picking the green beans from her monosodium glutamate Chinese dish and sniffing them.

Pathetic.

Later that night, as I lay on the top sheet of the bed next to Brian, scratching ferociously at the mosquito bites that had amassed behind my knees, I tried to determine what differentiated the perfect mother from me.

Why was she so perfect?

I concluded that her beauty and sereness must be the result of three things: dancing around the moon naked, drinking lots of wine, or taking regular yoga classes.

I knew I couldn't do the first. Not without being reported to the police. The second was proving impossible on our budget (plus, I don't think Indian people even know about grapes because if they did, why was there no sodding wine anywhere?), which left the third option. Yoga.

I let out a deep breath; stretched and lengthened my legs. Brian turned over. *Could I do it? Could I bend my body and cleanse my soul?* My torso felt rigid. The only stretchy part of me was my perineum. No matter. I could change. I *would* change. I promised myself, there and then, that when we left Gokarna, I would seek out a teacher and take up yoga.

I might even start drinking almond milk and taking a bath in cow piss, too.

Two days later. In the city of Udaipur

It was early morning. Leaving the kids slobbering in bed, Brian and I crept out to explore the local area. And that's when I saw it. The sign—propped up in front of a shabby-looking building—surrounded by dust and phlegm. "Yoga. Tonight 7 until 8".

Yes!

Giddy with excitement, I announced to Brian that I would attend the class every night for the duration of our stay. His shoulders slumped. He re-read the sign and turned to face me. Looking like a child whose cat had just been run over. 'Between seven and eight?' he whined. 'But what about the rum and Coke we always have before dinner? It's the only chance we get to have alcohol'.

Good point. Still. Surely any man in his right mind would prefer a wife who floated around in heavenly goodliness than one with shaky hands and whose teeth were rotting from too much sugary alcohol and soda?

I tossed my purple sarong over my shoulder and turned away dramatically. 'Let me do this. Please. It's something I need to do. For me, for you, for my body, for all of us'.

Brian wasn't listening.

He'd zoned out and was halfway down the street. Checking the football scores on his phone. Blowing into the USB port and shaking the device like a lunatic. Complaining that Sonny had used his charger with his dirty hands, and now his headphones didn't work properly.

As the day wore on, I became increasingly nervous about my pending yoga class. I even asked Tessa to come with me for support, suggesting we could have some yummy natural bonding time together. Mother and daughter. She declined. 'No thanks', she said a little too quickly. 'Tara Taylor's mum used to do yoga and said it was really freaky. Like the worst thing evv-er. All they did was sit around on mats all night talking about their wombs'.

Then she walked away and started laughing and whispering to Sonny.

Cruel. So cruel.

By the time 6.45 p.m. rolled around, I was all of a dither. It did cross my mind to give the whole thing a miss. To throw the yoga pants back into the dirty rucksack and pour some dark rum down my throat instead. That would make mummy a more beautiful person for sure. But no. 'Be strong, Liz', I said, opening my mouth wide in front of the mirror and checking for bits of curried chickpeas between my teeth.

I fixed a smile.

'You can do this. Think what you'll look like with smaller nipples'.

I knew. The minute I entered the whitewashed yoga class building, I knew I shouldn't have come. Something was off. Something wasn't right. My cosmic energy aura felt unaligned.

For a start, there were only two people there: me and a small Chinese boy. Who wasn't actually a boy but a man. And probably wasn't even Chinese.

I hovered in the doorway awkwardly, wishing I'd brought my phone.

The boy who wasn't a boy was preoccupied. Something seemed to be wrong with his shorts. He stood inside the room against the wall, fiddling with the drawstring around his waist. Fussing. Pulling the cord backwards and forwards until both ends were precisely even.

Maybe I should introduce him to Brian.

I tried not to stare. I picked my nail and remained in the doorway, deliberating whether or not having an obsessive-compulsive personality disorder meant that you didn't physically age.

The yoga room was square-shaped and smelled of stale incense. Two skinny windows set up high made it impossible to see in or out, and a wooden stained mahogany floor with a patterned oblong rug in the centre was scattered with a few decorative cushions and a wooden flute. There were two entrances. The one where I was standing and another at the back of the room. That one had a cardboard box propped up next to it with the words: "Donations welcome. Minimum 200 Rupees" scribbled on the front in red marker.

The boy with the symmetrical shorts looked at me. His eyes narrowed accusingly. I shuffled uncomfortably. *Maybe I'd stuffed up? Used the wrong entrance?* That would explain why the man-child was shunning me. He probably thought I was on the fiddle—a fiddler diddler. Out to swindle the Indian yoga society of two hundred rupees.

I walked into the room, faking confidence and stood by the pile of various coloured yoga mats stacked neatly against the wall. I tapped my chin pensively. Maybe I should give the naive boy-man a piece of advice? Explain to him that in the English language, the word "donation" means voluntary. As in, "only pay if you want to". And that, if he were sensible, like me, he would wait until the end of the class to pay. That way, he wouldn't get ripped off.

No. Best not.

Yoga is about forgiving and creating orgasmic sensations from the core, not about being a bossy boots who shares scams with foreigners.

I held my tongue. Still. I couldn't help but feel a pang of disappointment. *What a shame.* And there was me thinking that Chinese people were on their game when it came to business and stuff.

At 7.03 p.m., the back door swung open, and a man swept into the room. The Tutor. The Master. The Yogi Person. His long silver hair was secured neatly in a bun on top of his head, and he wore floor-skimming white robes. I noticed his eyes were heavily lined with black kohl pencil. He looked like David Bowie, only Indian.

Ignoring his small audience of two standing to the side, he sat down on the cushion in the centre of the room and closed his eyes. Through his dress, I could see that his legs were crossed. I couldn't quite tell if he was wearing any underpants.

I blushed and stood up straight. Reminding myself that I wouldn't be very good at Indian yoga if I continued to hunch next to the mats like a perverted peeping Tom. The body, after all, reflects that of the mind.

The master opened his eyes and inhaled deeply. Raising a smooth brown hand, he flittered his long fingers, inviting me and the juvenile to approach the rug. To come closer. To join him. Be as one. Us three.

'Aaahhhh', he exhaled.

There was a moment of awkwardness owing to the fact that the compulsive man-child couldn't decide which colour yoga mat to choose, but the tutor waited patiently. Serenely. I wanted to break the silence. Start a conversation. Ask the wizard how he intended to put his leg around his head while wearing a floor-length tunic. But I remained quiet. I wasn't sure if it was even called a tunic.

With all three seated, the class could finally begin.

I was ready. Psyched up and raring to stretch. I prepared myself for the moves by pulling my belly button in and clenching my bum cheeks. It is common knowledge that yoga people's navels are always tight.

I smiled and waited. And then waited some more.

Nothing.

No warm-ups, no stretches, no limbering. Nothing.

Then, silently and without warning, the yogi teacher reached for the wooden flute, lifted both elbows out to the side, pursed his lips and gently began to blow.

'Toooot-tooot-too-to-to-too-tooooott …'

What the?? I sat there. Stupefied.

While the wannabe flautist certainly looked the part, with his eyelids fluttering manically like an epileptic moth and his head doing that thing where it wobbles from side to side, the noise that came out was dire. Really crap. Tuneless and totally shite. I mean, I'm no Rachmaninoff, but I know a good tune when I hear one, and this was embarrassing.

I held my breath. Didn't know what to do. Where to look. I wasn't sure whether we were supposed to click our fingers in time to the music or sing along. It was toe-curling.

And to confuse matters, my eyes kept wandering to the bulge between his legs.

I did my best to relax. Drop my shoulders. But the flesh between my toes was suddenly hot and itchy, and I was desperate to scratch it. I arched my back and tried to push my chubby knees to the floor without tearing a ligament.

This was absurd.

Where were all the other Earth Mothers? Where were all the fathers with their bare chests and knobbly feet? Not here, that's for sure. No. There was just me, a Chinese man in a child's body, and the freak on a cushion. Dressed up like Gandhi with his eyes rolled back in his head—tooting.

What I wouldn't do for a rum and Coke.

I glanced at my watch. We'd been there for fifteen minutes and still hadn't moved a muscle.

What a rip-off.

The wee man-lad seemed to be enjoying the performance. He kept nodding furiously. Pointing at the wooden flute and smiling. Maybe it was a Chinese song.

Eventually, the pied piper stopped and lay down the flute. I watched as his dark eyes scanned the room. He seemed agitated.

Annoyed. Miffed that the only people there to witness his freak show were a mature infant and a middle-aged perv with athlete's foot.

I pressed my palms to the floor in a conscious effort not to clap.

People who come to yoga don't applaud the flute player, you idiot. They're too in the moment.

The tutor stared straight ahead. He seemed to be thinking about something really important. Waiting for a vision. Or maybe another two hundred rupees to walk through the door. No one said a word. The aged juvenile nodded. At what, I don't know.

The smell of incense was starting to make me feel sick. I felt uncomfortable. Awkward. Maybe this silence thing was some sort of test—a cruel joke. Let's see who breaks first; the old woman or the Chinese street urchin. My mind wandered. I had questions, so many questions. *How did the yogi master keep his robes so white in a town built on dust? Did he use a top-loading washing machine or just give it a swill in the river along with the rest of India? What brand eyeliner was he wearing?*

Finally, he spoke.

'Go home', soothed the teacher's voice. 'Go home now'.

At first, I thought it was all part of the show. A cow-like, Buddha-like ritual that all yoga tutors say to first-timers. So I didn't move. I looked over to Beijing boy, who seemed distressed. He was frowning at the rug on the floor. One of the corners had accidentally folded over on itself.

'Go home', repeated the tutor; this time, his tone more impatient. He tilted his chiselled chin towards the exit.

Still, I remained. Smiling like a half-wit. Nodding like a twat. Waiting for something to happen. Poised on my mat, ready for the next act.

The yogi master got to his feet. He reached down and snatched the wooden flute. 'You go home now. You come back tomorrow when more people be here'. And with that, he left.

Well. How rude. How bloody fucking rude.

I wanted to protest. Get up and run after the trickster. Grab hold of his bony shoulders, spin him around and scream into his face, 'Listen here, Mr Mystic! I've waited a long time for this. My family and I have trekked across the Rajasthan Desert to get here. And him? That little man-boy with problems? He's already paid his two hundred rupees'.

But I didn't.

Instead, I flew out of the building with sprouted wings. Ran along the dusty road to our one-star hotel and climbed the steep stairs that led to our room.

And there it was.

The light of my life. My treasure. My beloved. The one thing guaranteed to make Mummy flowy and calm, and lubricated.

A glass of Indian rum and Coke held by a man with a sweaty belly and a beautiful smile.

Namaste, my love. Namaste.

CHAPTER SIX
THAILAND

If you take the train from Bangkok and keep going North for about seven hundred kilometres, you'll come to Chiang Mai, the largest city in Northern Thailand.

Chiang Mai is divine. Both cosmopolitan and refreshingly Asian. The city is built on the banks of the Ping River and is surrounded by mountains, rice fields, and lush countryside. The air is hot and humid and smells of jasmine, ginger, and lemongrass, and at sunrise, a magical mist looms in the valleys of the moody mountain ranges dominating the skyline.

Although there are many districts in Chiang Mai, it helps my brain to think of the city as being split into two parts (anything more than that, and I get confused).

First, there is the old walled city, founded more than seven hundred years ago and surrounded by a beautiful moat. This part of Chiang Mai is eclectic and charming, with temples and markets and characterful accommodation that fills up quickly with tourists.

And then there is Nimmanhaemin. Or Nim, if you are young and hip like me.

Nim is the student area of Chiang Mai. It is trendy and up-and-coming. Here you will find the vast university, a couple of swanky malls, and plenty of air-conditioned cafés which act as offices for digital nomads who spend their days drinking Macha lattes and orgasming over the speed of the internet.

Accommodation in and around Nim is cheaper than in the old city. Considerably cheaper. Which is why we stayed there (obviously). And when you don't have to pay as much for your digs, you can spend the excess money on other stuff. Like hiring bikes. Which is fun.

Apparently.

Not long after arriving in Chiang Mai, the lady who owned the Airbnb asked us if we wanted to rent some bikes.

As a side note, this multi-service offering is common practice in Thailand. Side hustles are huge. Everyone's at it. Even the bloke in the mall who sold us the black charger lead for our laptop asked Brian if he wanted to pop into his backroom for a wet shave and a ball wax.

Our landlady's name was Dao. It's hard to say how old Dao was. Sixty maybe? I don't know, and I didn't like to ask. She had waist-length black hair that was flecked with grey and parted through the middle. She reminded me of Yoko Ono. Only rounder. And without the thick eyebrows and weird hats.

Compared to my practically non-existent Thai, Dao's English was excellent. When she spoke, her voice was soft and sing-song-like.

But there was no hiding this woman's true nature.

Dao was a battle-axe. I could tell. I knew within a few hours of being there when she scolded me for putting Sonny's trainers in the tumble drier. I said to myself: *this here is a wolf in sheep's clothing. A Yoko Ono-looking wolf dollied up as a fluffy Thai sheep. It takes one to know one. There's no tricking me.*

Dao's main residence and ours were separated only by a low hedge of shrubs. Meaning that I could spy on her whenever I had nothing better to do. More than once, I'd witnessed her pegging out her frilly knickers on the rotary washing line. Rubbing her hands together at the thought of how much money she was saving on electricity.

One morning, while I was walking around the garden pretending to admire the dead grass, Dao called to me from over the hedge.

'Hey Yo! Good morning!' came the cheery voice, accompanied by a toothy smile. 'You want rent my good bikes for some good sightseeing?'

(Dao liked the word good. She used it a lot.)

She obviously took the wrinkle on my forehead to mean yes, and before I knew it, there she was. At the end of the driveway holding a two-wheeled bone-shaker between her knobbly knees. Nodding. At nothing.

As it happened, the day before, I'd suggested to Brian that we should think about hiring some bikes; be like proper tourists. We'd even stopped at the little place down the road and enquired about the price. But that's as far as we'd gone. Brian said the owner of the shop reminded him of a drug dealer he knew in the '80s, so we went home. By foot.

'You like?' came the rhetorical and loaded-with-impatience question. Dao looked at me and nodded. Again.

I turned my back and scanned the house for Brian. Nowhere to be seen.

Shit. Nothing like a bit of pressure to start the day.

I won't lie; I'm not a fan of bikes. Me and them have a bit of a dark history.

When I was twelve, I borrowed my brother's Grifter without asking and left it parked outside the shop while I nipped in to get a Wham bar. When I came out, the bike was gone. Nicked. My dad went mad and insisted I pay for my crime. For a whole year, I had to deposit 50p a week into my brother's NatWest Piggy Account. It put me off bikes for ages. I wouldn't have minded, but the bloody thing was a second-hand Christmas present. It must have been worth all of about ten quid.

But this was Thailand. And everyone knows that cycling in Asia is fun.

Determined not to be ripped off and hoping to get some sort of long-term discount, I bravely informed Dao that we'd be renting the bikes for the duration of our stay.

'We're here for a month … so …' I swallowed back my British fear and reminded myself that asking for a discount wasn't rude; it was business-like. 'Could you quite possibly knock the price down—'

Wolfy was having none of it.

'Two dollar a day', she snapped. 'Each. This best good price'. Then she held out the antique bike with an outstretched arm and admired it adoringly. I half expected her to perform some sort of circus act. Do a handstand on the seat and flash her lady parts to the passing traffic.

I blew the air from my cheeks and retracted my chin, causing it to triple. *Pshht.* The price seemed a bit hefty to me. Two dollars a day could keep me and Bri in Chang beer for a week.

Clueless and awkward, I pinched the back tyre of the bike and fiddled with the spokes. I stared at the cracked fake leather seat for a few minutes, frowned at God knows what, and then eventually (after running out of bike parts to touch), I rubbed my chin, and tried to look detached like one of those men who sit at the back of auction houses wagging their finger because they no longer want to bid.

'The bike shop down the road only charges one dollar fifty a day…' My voice cracked. I coughed nervously and shifted my weight from one foot to the other.

Dao's nostrils flared. Her pupils doubled in size. I thought for a moment her head might explode.

'They. No. Basket'. Steely voice. Ice cold stare. *Battle-axe.*

Negotiations ended there. I paid the money, and within the hour, four crappy bikes were parked outside our front door.

I've never had much luck buying clothes in Asia.

The tops have huge gaping armholes that make you look like you have an elephant growth hanging from your pits, and the pants always, without fail, come apart at the crutch.

No exaggeration.

Every single pair of trousers I have ever purchased in Asia has lasted me no more than a week. By day seven, the stitching between the legs frays and splays. Don't ask me why; I have no clue. Either somebody is playing a cruel joke on me, or my bum cheeks are inflating by the hour.

The only positive to this Asian haberdashery error is that whenever I wear these pants, a consistent breeze wafts from the outside world through to my knickers. Which lowers my temperature and chills me out. Provides me with my very own fanny fridge. Which is why I have never returned a pair of the shoddy pants to the seller and demanded a refund. They may not know it, but the tailors of Asia have unearthed the solution to every perimenopausal woman's nightmare. Cooling the hot flush from below.

It was early evening. The sun in Chiang Mai had gone down ten minutes earlier, and the temperature was at that perfect stage. Still warm enough to go out without a cardy but cool enough not to sweat buckets when you do anything more strenuous than itch your head.

The four of us stood in the Airbnb's small kitchen. Hovering between the toaster and the fridge. Trying to decide how we'd spend the evening.

'Let's take our bikes and explore the city!' Brian suggested. He grinned and drummed his fingers against the Formica countertop like a passionate pianist finishing up a concerto; waiting for the audience to erupt into applause. Sonny and Tessa nodded approvingly.

Borr-ring.

I slouched onto the countertop.

The thought of biking around the city and pretending to like it left me cold. I'd rather go to the café at the end of the street and eavesdrop on that couple from Manchester. The ones who spend hours arguing about the interest free loan he borrowed from her dad at Easter.

'Ohhh! Yes! Good idea, Daddy! Can we, Mummy? Pleeease?' Tessa's eyes were as wide as saucers. She fiddled excitedly with the box of Lipton tea bags that had been left out on the counter and were now home to a million ants. 'That would be such good fun! And I bet Daddy could lead us to that park with the badminton courts'.

Brian arched his back and cracked his knuckles.

Sometimes, I wanted to gag that girl and throw her into a rat-infested cellar.

'Fine', I said mardily. 'I'll go. But we're not playing badminton'. I flicked her hand with a tea towel. 'And stop touching the teabags with your germy hands. It's disgusting'.

It's boiling hot in Thailand. Far too hot to wear a bra. That's why whenever you see social media posts of women strolling along white sandy beaches in Phuket or prancing around at one of those mental health retreats with a bunch of weird hippies from Ibiza, none of them is wearing a bra. Because it's Too. Bloody. Hot.

(It's also a well-known fact that spirituality flows faster through bare breasts.)

Unfortunately, there was to be no beach strolling or jungle masturbating for me.

Not a chance.

I am the wife of Brian, whose idea of a sexy woman is Margaret Thatcher in twin-set and pearls, and am the mother of two teenagers who die of embarrassment if you mention menstrual flow. I couldn't possibly risk my family seeing my nip-naps bare and unclothed. No. If I wanted to go braless in Thailand, I'd have to think of something genius.

And so I did.

It was called wearing my huge purple kaftan. The one I bought in India. The one that makes me look like the lesbian art teacher who used to teach pottery to reformed criminals at the local community college. I love my kaftan because I can wear it without a bra. Which is comfy and wonderfully liberating. It is loose and flowy and covered in a messy paisley pattern, making it impossible to detect any sign of human body shape. I would challenge anyone, even a lech who spends their days fiddling with their down belows, to point out where my knockers start and my belly ends.

Whenever I wear my purple kaftan, Brian frowns.

'Why don't we go and find you a pretty dress to buy at the market?' he suggests. 'A white one with buttons. A nice long one'.

Knob head.

'How thoughtful of you, darling', I say, swishing my kaftan from side to side like Shirley Temple. 'Maybe tomorrow. But definitely not today. Kaftans are for real women with oblong udders and clay-stained hands'.

While the rest of the family was outside preparing for our forthcoming bike ride, checking chains and lowering saddles, I stood alone in the bedroom. Trying to decide if it was absolutely necessary for me to take off my kaftan and strap myself into a bra.

I'm not stupid. Even I know that going braless on a bike ride is an accident waiting to happen. What if I pulled on the brakes and accidentally pinched my dangling nipples?

Ouch. I could see it now.

Swerving into the oncoming traffic, laying hobbled on the road. My poor children being made to come and identify me. Tessa, having to admit that, 'Yes, that is indeed my mother. And oh. My. God. How embarrassing. She is clutching her tit'.

My nostril hair fizzed, and my heart raced. I sat down on the bed and tried to recall the last time my teats had been tweaked.

It was sixteen years ago. When Sonny was three weeks old. I was still breastfeeding and wanted to go to the cinema with my sister-in-law. Leave baby at home with daddy. I hooked myself up to one of those lactation machines you could rent from Mothercare for thirty quid and milked myself. Brian was sitting next to me on the couch. Muted. Watching in horror as his wife's once pert nipples were yanked, sucked and twisted like a piece of old plasticine.

And all for a thimble full of breastmilk and a film that was shite.

I took off my faithful kaftan and replaced it with my black sports bra. The one with the crossover straps. I pulled it over my head and stood sideways to the mirror, patting my belly. It rippled. *Not bad for a woman who hated exercise and ate the same size food portions as her husband.*

Tessa liked it when I wore this bra. She approved. She said it made me look like one of those sporty mothers who wore their hair in a ponytail and did Pilates after school drop-off. I threw on a tee-shirt and adjusted the drawstring of my Asian pants. I was ready. All set to go.

I knew it would happen. It always does.

Whenever we go on a bike ride, my family thinks it perfectly acceptable to cycle ahead and leave me behind. Trailing at the back like a tosser.

I watched helplessly as the three of them stood up on their pedals and sped away. Leaving me in a cloud of dust. Wobbling precariously on a contraption one up from a penny-farthing. It wasn't until they'd reached the end of the street that they even realised I was no longer with them.

I saw Brian turn his head and do some sort of thumb gesture over his shoulder, and then seconds later, Sonny cruised back down the street towards me. His blonde hair blowing in the breeze. His cheeks glowing with joyfulness. Smiling good-naturedly like Julian from the *Famous Five*.

'Come on, slowcoach!' He pedalled around the back of me like a shepherd herding up a goat with foot rot. 'Get a move on!'

I squinted like a crow and pushed my tongue into the side of my cheek.

People in Thailand don't shout. It's not like in India, where everyone sounds as though they're having a domestic when actually, all they're doing is asking for a cup of chai.

No.

Thai people are calm. Beautiful and serene (apart from Dao, of course), but other than her, Thai people are placid. They don't throw their arms in the air and screech at their children while they're riding their bikes, for example. No. They'd never do that.

But I'm not Thai.

A young girl in a school uniform was walking across the street opposite, drinking pink bubble tea through a straw. Watching us with wide eyes. I waited for her to pass.

'I'll tell you what, boy', I spluttered like an overfilled kettle. 'You shouldn't be on that bloody bike'. I wiped the sweat from my right palm across my knee, causing the thin front wheel to wobble. 'Instead of trying to look like a cool dude, why don't you try using some hand signals to tell me where you're going? You won't look so clever when you're laying in a hospital bed, dead and covered in blood, will you?'

There. That should do it.

That should put an end to this happy-go-lucky attitude. Send Julian crying back to George and Timmy the dog. I regained my balance and pushed ahead, commending myself on my imaginative and progressive parenting techniques.

Sonny didn't respond. He cruised alongside me, looking straight ahead. His gaze relaxed. One hand resting on the handlebar and the other in his lap. The gap between us expanded.

Cocky little swine.

He could think again if he thought I was going to let him take his driving test when we got back to New Zealand. *No way. Not happening.* He wouldn't be getting behind the wheel of any car until he'd learned how to ride a bike safely around the supermarket playground and achieved his cycling proficiency certificate. The one that sticks on the fridge.

I raised my elbows out to the side and heaved down on my thighs, refusing to be left behind again. I puffed out my cheeks and shook my head profusely. Muttering like a madwoman at every passing car that came within two meters of me.

A childhood memory flashed into my mind.

I was sitting on my grandma's lap in the front room of her semi-detached house in Lancashire. We were watching *The Adventures of Noddy* together and eating Joe's Mint Balls. I remember the programme as clear as day. It was the episode where Big Ears went loopy and chased Noddy around the town on his bike. I'm pretty sure he was threatening to kill him with a knife.

Nong Buak Haad Public Park is located in the Southwest corner of Chiang Mai's old city. It is open every day from dusk until dawn and offers visitors and locals the chance to relax within its beautiful green surroundings. There are landscaped gardens, ponds, bridges, lush flowerbeds, and fountains that look far too posh for Thailand. There is also an outside gym where fit, strong people go to flex their muscles and show off their bods.

'Ooh, look', cried Tessa as we pushed our bikes across a pedestrian crossing and headed towards the park entrance. 'There are exercise machines and everything! Fun!'

Sometimes I wonder how different life would be if my daughter was a Goth who sat in a dark room all day playing Dungeons and Dragons.

We wheeled our bikes to an area where others were parked, and I dismounted the saddle with about as much grace as a three-toed sloth. 'Ooowwwch', I moaned dramatically as I guided my knee over the back wheel and plonked my foot to the ground. My pubic bone felt as though it had been melted down, put onto a blacksmith's anvil and hammered to within an inch of its life. I kicked out the rusty bike stand and watched as my bike toppled over. Taking Brian's and a bunch of other bikes with it. Then I pouted like a codfish and hobbled away.

While Brian and Sonny headed for the big boy pull-up bars, Tessa and I made our way towards the bright orange inner thigh machine that sat menacingly in the corner of the park under a tree.

Don't ask me why we did this; to this day, I have no idea. Maybe I saw it as the chance to claw back some fitness credibility; make up for the humiliation I had experienced by being the one left behind on the bike ride. I'd show my daughter how to pump iron. I might even join in with the free aerobic session taking place on the other side of the park. I was wearing my sports bra, after all.

Tessa had never seen a machine like this before. One that worked the inner thighs. She stood sensibly to the side, reading the instructions that were written in English while I pushed past her like Mad Lizzie from TV AM.

This was my territory. Mummy's turn now.

I stepped up and settled into the deep bucket seat that was smooth and worn from years of use. Tessa turned to face me. The seat tilted back with my weight, and the eye-level handlebars designed to hold you in place fell down with a thump and flattened my chest. I let out a slow grunty breath and began opening and lifting my legs.

'Oh, Mummy. Be careful …. I don't think you're supposed to use it like that ….'

Silly girl. She obviously didn't know that I had watched Jamie-Lee Curtis in *Perfect* about fifteen times and knew everything there was to know about toning flab.

After a bit of heaving, lifting, and strategic manoeuvring, I managed to wrap my thighs around the machine. My legs were in place. Fanned out. Spread. Tessa's eyes widened. Her cheeks blushed. She took two steps backwards. 'Are you sure you don't want me to get Daddy?'

'Don't worry, darling', I said reassuringly, using the same voice as Mary Poppins when she talked to Jane and Michael. 'Me and this machine have been friends for years. Watch me. All you have to do is gently s-q-u-e-e-z-e'.

Nothing happened. Diddly squat. Not a thing. I lifted my chin and tried again.

'That's right. You just s-q-u-e-e-z-e your knees together against the machine, and s-l-o-w-l-y bring your thighs together'. Zilch. *Sod all.*

Tessa stood.

Poised.

Watching.

Waiting for something to happen.

She didn't have to speak. Her eyes said it all. *Please, God, get my mother off that machine, and please, please don't let there be anyone watching. And also why am I not a Goth?*

I strained to bring my legs together. A trickle of urine escaped down my thigh. Hot. Wet. I was stuck. Pinned on the shiny orange machine with my legs bent outwards at a 90-degree angle. Like a frog in labour. A frog whose waters had just broken.

Snorting air from my nostrils I bounced my legs like a human space hopper, hoping the machine would budge and release me from this hideous undignified position. 'It doesn't … work', I wheezed. 'It's seized up'.

Tessa pulled at a bit of loose thread on her denim shorts. She glanced over her shoulder nervously.

Thankfully, Brian had his back to me. He was busy showing Sonny the difference between a pull-up and a chin-up and telling him how old Sylvester Stallone was when he made *Rocky III*. I swallowed a dry nothing and tried to remain calm. As calm as a woman with her legs jammed open on a machine in the middle of a public park in Thailand can be.

'It's bloody well broken', I gasped. The veins bulged in my neck. My legs remained spread. I began to flap around like a chicken avoiding a horny rooster.

Another childhood memory sprang to mind.

When I was seven, I had a friend who owned a tortoise. I say friend, really we were more like acquaintances. She was rich and her parents owned the local fruit and veg shop, and I was poor and lived in a council house with an outside toilet. Looking back, I think she only played with me because she was starved of junk food, and I'd let her share my Primula cheese sandwiches at tuck time.

One afternoon, me and my friend were playing outside, and she got called in for her tea. Her mum said that I could wait for her in the garden. After ten minutes of waiting, I became bored, so I walked over to the enclosure where the tortoise lived and lifted him out. Sneakily, I carried my captive to a patch of grass that couldn't be seen from the house, and I lay him down on his back. To see what would happen. *I know. What can I say? I must have been a child sadist with we-never-had-money-for-a-pet issues.*

I watched in fascination as the helpless ancient tortoise blinked his leathery eyelids and wriggled around in a panic. Unable to flip itself over. Its little claw legs turning in circles. Writhing around in vain.

And now here I was.

Forty-one years later. Receiving payback from the Thai Goddess of Reptile Worshippers.

'Help me, Tessa. Help me get out of this seat. Stop looking at Daddy, and help me! NOW!'

My heart pounded desperately. A pool of sweat collected between my boobs. My bra itched. Hot, prickly, embarrassed tears threatened their way to the corners of my eyes. I was trapped. Forever. *Kill me now*. Nothing could be worse than this.

And then it happened.

The embarrassment of all embarrassments.

Rrrrrrrrpppppp.

The Asian pants gave way.

'Ewww mummy … That's gross!' Tessa shrieked, burying her head in her hands and hiding her eyes coyly in a way that only a thirteen-year-old girl can do. She peeked through her fingers and giggled. I made a mental note to lobby for the return of smacking when I got back to New Zealand. 'There's a massive rip in your pants, and your knickers are all sticking out and … Ewww … how embarrassing … they're … they're …wet!'

You're alright, Liz. You're okay. Just breathe. They're clean, at least.

Thailand is famous for monasteries and monks. For practising meditation and living off fresh air. I tried to recall the technique I'd read about while sitting on the toilet the week before. The one that encourages gratitude. To think of every experience, both good and bad, as a reason to be thankful.

I closed my eyes and began. *Okay. Here goes.*

I'm thankful it's nearly dark, and the park isn't crowded with tourists.

I'm thankful a queue of local people isn't waiting to use this machine.

I'm thankful I'm stuck on this machine and, therefore, cannot be done for child abuse.

And fuck me … I am thankful for the cool breeze that's blowing through my knickers.

CHAPTER SEVEN
VIETNAM

What's not to love about Vietnam? Home to rice terraces, beautiful beaches and spectacular landscapes. Vietnam. Where nobody seems to be in a rush, but everyone has somewhere to go. Vietnam. Where the people are kind and patient and will light up your day with their smiles.

Mostly.

No one likes to be done over. Had. Taken for a ride down a primrose lane.

There's only one ride you should experience in Vietnam, and that's on a bicycle. The sort with two wheels and a saddle. Unless, of course, you're part of one of those #noregrets tours, in which case, you'll probably get to ride Tam. The shaggy-haired surfer from Queensland who stands at the front of the bus yelling about how trippy and facking aw-sooooome the Nam is.

Bike riding is a way of life in Vietnam. Everyone does it. So much so that our twenty dollars-a-night Airbnb included four bikes as part of the deal. It's true that they were a bit ropey and crap, and yes, one of them looked like something the grandad from *Chitty Chitty Bang Bang* had made, but who cares? Free is free. Free is good. We like free.

We loved riding our bikes in Vietnam. Pedalling along with the masses. Feeling like locals. Weaving in and out of the traffic that came from this way and that, crossing, swerving, speeding up, slowing down.

You'd think with so many bikes on the road, someone would collide, but they don't. The Vietnamese are very skilled and courteous cyclists. Throughout our stay, we didn't see one accident. Not one. Which made the whole experience even more pleasurable. It gives you a real sense of achievement when you flop into bed at night, knowing that you and your family have managed to avoid being obliterated or run over.

Hoi An is an ancient city located in Vietnam's central Quang Nam Province. It's about nine hundred km north of Ho Chi Minh and eight hundred km south of Hanoi. If you are looking for Hoi An on a map, it's the one halfway up by the sea.

The old quarter in Hoi An is exquisite. Really lovely. Paper lanterns of every shade are strung across the streets, bobbing provocatively in the warm breeze. Pretty cerise-coloured flowers climb over doorways, and local shopkeepers wave and smile, enticing you to browse their offerings. It's all very fairy tale-ish. Like being on one of those Disneyland rides. The ones with the boats that go really slow, and you're glad to be on them because your feet are killing you.

It's only when you blink and notice a massive fish head or a stall full of cheap Tiger Balm that you remember you're in Asia and not in some Floridian made-up world dancing with pink glittery octopuses.

When we were in Thailand, we met a British guy in a 7-Eleven. He asked us where we were visiting next, and when we told him Vietnam, a smile spread across his face.

'You'll love it', he said.

And he was right. We did. Vietnam left us with nothing but good memories.

All apart from one.

It was a gloriously sunny day, and because I am an outdoorsy and fun kind of mother who wishes she belonged to one of those healthy families that cycle from Bristol to Cheddar Gorge for something to do on a Sunday, I suggested to the kids that we ride our bikes to the local beach. Take an outing.

'Oh no … r-e-a-l-l-y? Why can't we go to that baguette place and then come back here and watch the *Avengers* trilogy on the iPad?' whined my oldest child, lurching and groaning as if I'd just suggested he eat his own liver.

Sometimes I wonder if my son was swapped at birth. Given to me by mistake.

The beach was approximately four miles from where we were staying. If we got a wiggle on, we could be down on the sand in time for lunch. I voiced my thoughts to the kids making sure to emphasise the word "lunch".

'What? We're going to go to a proper café?' They sprung up like a pair of meerkats. 'A real one?'

I smiled inwardly at their stupidness.

Silly children.

Everyone knows that cafés on beaches are a rip-off and that a bag of thirty-cent spicy Cheetos from the local stall is more than sufficient for lunch.

I gathered together a few heavy essentials and popped them into Brian's backpack. 'We'll see', I lied, trotting around the apartment and opening all the curtains. 'Oh, and don't anyone bother bringing a ChapStick. I'm going to carry one for all of us to use'.

April is the best month to visit Vietnam. It hardly ever rains, and the temperature is just right. Not too hot or humid. Perfect for bike riding.

That morning, while pedalling along the very straight and never-ending road with my happy-go-lucky family, I noticed an old farmer taking his cow for a stroll. Leading it along a rocky path that bordered some paddy fields. Probably taking it to a market to swap for some beans or something.

'Ohh, look!' I screeched, taking my hand off the handlebars and almost causing the first-ever pile-up in the history of Hoi An. 'A man with a Vietnamese hat on!'

I know. In Vietnam. Who'd have thought?

The dense green paddy fields were set below the road, meaning that to get to the man, we would have to stop and climb down a bank.

Because I am a demented, menopausal half-wit who is always on the lookout for ways to ruin calm and pleasant days, I chose not to cycle on my merry way and instead suggested that we stop and talk to the straw local and his cow. Get a picture.

'What do you think?' I called out in high spirits, pleased at being the one to spot the one-man circus. 'Shall we go and stroke the man's cow and twizzle his tail?'

Tessa and Brian exchanged glances.

'Oh my God, REALLY… Can we just not?' Sonny let out a huge sigh and shook his head. His lank, sweaty hair clung to the sides of his cheeks like strands of soggy seaweed. 'If I stop, my chain will come off. It always does'. He was pedalling backwards furiously. 'I hate this bike. This bike is rubbish. Why did I have to have *this* bike …?'

I steered onto the verge, leaving my son ranting to himself in the middle of the road, pedalling around in circles like Dougal from *The Magic Roundabout*. 'Stupid bike! I told you not to stop … (huff) … Why is the chain so loose? Why … (bash) … do I … (clang) have to have this bike …. Why can't we be like a normal family and gets Ubers and stuff…?'

* You know earlier how I told you we all loved riding our bikes? I lied. Sonny drew the short straw and got the duffer bike. We never heard the end of it.

Funny, isn't it? Whenever you're in the middle of a family crisis, an audience suddenly appears. It's at times like this when I seriously question the made-upness of *The Truman Show*.

From out of nowhere, a man and a woman came cycling towards us. Tourists whizzing along effortlessly on brand-spanking new bikes.

All teeth and tans. Fresh and cool in their white Airtex tee-shirts and Birkenstock sandals. The smell of cologne wafted through the air as they swerved to miss my son, who was zig-zagging all over the road on his possessed bike, not watching where he was going. I smiled apologetically and waved them on their way. Feeling important, like PC Plod. *Move along, please. Nothing to see. No demon teen here.*

I waited for the bikers to get out of earshot then I shouted across the road to my son irritably. 'Just drop it into fifth gear! And then keep clicking that thing on the left-hand side until the chain is on the smallest bit in the middle'.

Christ. Beryl Burton, eat your heart out.

'You're forgetting, Liz', mumbled Brian as he threw his bike onto the side of the road and pushed past me to rescue our son. 'That *his* bike is the one with no gears'.

Looking back now, I should have picked up that the Vietnamese cow farmer was far too eager to take my photo.

Leaving my bike propped up against a tree at the side of the road, I turned to my family and offered them one last chance to experience a Vietnamese extraordinaire. 'Are you sure you don't want to come and meet the man and his cow?' I asked, secretly hoping they would say no so I could enjoy all the attention.

'You go', said Brian, looking for somewhere to wipe the oil from his hands. 'We'll wait here'.

'Yes, you go, Mummy', added Tessa, folding her arms across her chest and sticking out her hip like a double jointed Barbie doll. She half turned to her brother and muttered from the corner of her mouth, 'She's only doing it to put it on Facebook. It's always the same'.

The three of them huddled together and watched as I clambered down the steep bank towards the fields, stunned that I was actually going to go through with it.

'Be careful, Mummy!' came a last-minute panicky voice. *Ha. Too late.*

I advanced slowly towards the stranger and his cow. Never once turning back to say goodbye. Eyes facing forward.

Like Carol Anne walking into the telly.

The farmer and his beast hadn't gotten far. They were standing to the side of the next rice field along, lingering. Loitering. Almost as if they were waiting for me. The cow pushed small stones around with its muzzle while the man fiddled with his hat and picked his nose. *How lucky!* I thought. *I've caught them just in the nick of time.*

Holding my phone in one hand and pointing enthusiastically at the fly-infested beast with the other, I opened my mouth as wide as it would go and mouthed silently like one of those junior school hymn teachers with abnormally flexible lips. 'P-h-o-t-o? Photo of me and the …'

Lickety-split came the reply.

'Vang! Vang! Vang! Vang!'

The old man nodded eagerly. Bouncing his head up and down like one of those springy dog ornaments on a car dashboard. He flashed a toothless grin and slapped one knee. *Crikey. It didn't take much to convince this one.*

I lowered my head coyly and pressed my palms together. 'Thank you', I gushed, sneaking a look back up to the kids to see if they were watching. Annoyingly they had their backs turned, deeply engrossed in a game of paper, scissors, rock. The cow raised its head and snorted

Fools. They'd regret missing out on this one-off opportunity.

Surprisingly, the old farmer man wasn't fazed by the task of organising a photo shoot. He seemed quite prepared. Rather than have me pose next to the cow, he pointed to its back. Laying his little brown satchel on the ground, he crouched down and held out his interlinked fingers for me to stand on.

Gosh. What a gentleman.

I lifted my right foot into the waiting hands and grabbed onto the side of the cow for support. *He-eaa-vv-ve.* The old codger flinched as his arthritic joints cracked. He let out a small cry as his hands gave way.

'Oh, my goodness, I'm so sorry!' I blushed, stepping down quickly and attempting to giggle like a schoolgirl in the hope that I sounded cute and not cackily like one of those raucous old hags you see staggering up the street on New Year's Eve. 'I might look tiny, but I actually have surprisingly big bones'.

I popped my pinky finger into the corner of my mouth and blinked a big blink.

The old man looked confused and somewhat terrified. Massaging his swollen knuckles and jabbering a string of words under his breath, he turned me around, sunk his fingers deep into my dimply thighs and then threw me up onto the cow like a sack of old potatoes.

How exciting. It's not often I get to straddle a horned beast.

'Look at me!' I wanted to shout. 'I'm on top of a cow, and his fur is all shiny and slippery!' But no one was watching or listening, so I twisted my wedding ring around on my finger and stayed silent.

Handing the farmer my phone, I struck my first pose. Making sure to push my elbows out so that my bat wings wouldn't show.

Snap, snap, snap. Click, click, click. This way, that way, anyway you want way.

Thirty-eight photos were taken in total. All of me with my legs splayed across the farmer's livelihood.

Me lying on the cow. Me stroking the cow's neck. Me pouting at the cow. One between the ears of the cow. One from behind the tail. I think he even took one of me pretending to be asleep on the effing thing. I felt like Christie Brinkley when she posed naked with that black horse, and the animal rights mob went berserk.

With the publicity stunt over and the novelty wearing thin, things started to feel awkward. A bit like when you say goodbye to someone in the supermarket and then meet them again at the checkout.

'I'll let you get on your way', I said, suddenly aware of how old and silly I must look. I smoothed the cow's fur gratefully and looked over at my family. They were playing a game of slaps. Lowering their hands and screaming hysterically every time the other managed to rap their skin.

My heart skipped a beat. I wished I was with them. The ground suddenly seemed a long way down.

With about as much grace as a harbour Seal lolloping into the sea, I dismounted. God knows how I did it, but I did. I straightened myself up and patted the cow like a donkey, then I thanked the farmer and turned to leave.

And *this* was where things went horribly wrong.

The old man, who minutes earlier was snapping away happily like Ansel Adams, now stood in my way menacingly. Blocking my path. His face had changed. Morphed. Gone was the kind, toothless smile, and in its place, a weirdly psychotic and slightly mental grin. Like Zippy from *Playschool* when he's up to mischief and decides to surprise Bungle by revealing his furry penis.

'Dollars', came the demand in perfect English. A hand with dirty creases was thrust under my nose. 'American dollars. For photo'.

The smile had vanished. Along with the nodding head. No leeway. No kindness. Nothing. Just mean and scowling and big.

Damn. I hadn't seen that one coming. If I'd known it was a paid service, I'd have asked for proper lighting.

Reminding myself that the man was just trying to make a living and consoling myself with the fact that if I paid for this, I wouldn't have to give to charity for at least another thirty years, I reached into my back pocket and took out the cat purse. The one that held our emergency money. In it was a five-dollar note.

No Cheetos today, kids.

*We had been told before we arrived in Vietnam that carrying American dollars is advisable. There are a lot of accommodations, for example, that will only take American dollars as payment. We found this to be true in the stilt house where we stayed in Mai Chau. The owner made us walk twenty minutes up the street to exchange our Dong for dollars at the local bank. And it was raining.

Smiling weakly, I swallowed back the excess saliva that had filled up my mouth and handed the money to the angry-looking man. *There. Have your money and release me, you thug.* I turned to go.

'Not ENOUGH!' shouted the farmer. Pointing to my purse, his eyes filled with rage. 'The price FIFTY dollars!'

My skin prickled. *Fifty dollars? Fifty effing dollars? What planet was this man on?*

'Fifty dollars! You pay! NOW!!' His voice was loud. Angry. Pissed off.

My heart thumped. I wanted to call out, but the words wouldn't leave my mouth. The man held his stare. The cow stomped its foot.

Fuck.

It's annoying, isn't it? Whenever you try to do something in secret or want a bit of privacy, the whole world and their dog can't take their eyes off you. Yet the minute you get into a spot of trouble and need someone's actual attention because you are having a real-life-can-you-please-help-me emergency, there's no one around.

And not only that, but your husband decides to turn into Stuart Hall and host the most epic game of slaps in the history of man.

I bored my eyes into Brian's back. Nothing. He was close enough to see me but too far away to hear what was being said. Anyway, even if he was looking, which he wasn't, he'd assume I was just having a friendly conversation with the countryman. Telling him how many followers I had on Pinterest.

I froze, imagining my own funeral. Brian crying. Tessa motherless. Sonny pushing a bike with ribbons on the handlebars. I could see the headlines: 'Innocent and Very Attractive Woman Clobbered to Death by Vietnamese Dick Turpin and His Accomplice Evil Steed. And all so she could show off on Instagram'.

A pool of sweat soaked my armpits.

Sometimes, you meet certain people, don't you? You might pass them in the street or in a shop, and you know, you know that your paths will one day cross again. I'm not sure how you know this; you just do. I think it has something to do with the ether or yoga or something like that. Remember the two tourists I told you about earlier? The ones who swerved to miss Sonny on his bike?

Suddenly, I heard voices.

American voices—loud upstate New York accent voices. The voices of tourists thrilled to have spotted a real-life Vietnamese farmer wearing a hat and holding a cow on a rope.

'Jaaaake! Honey! Stooop! Come back here and look at this!'

I lifted my head towards the road.

It was them! The two cyclists. The tourists with the shiny bikes and teeth. The couple who earlier had been so intent on not crashing into my son on his gearless bike had completely missed Bunco Bill and Mama Moo taking a stroll in the paddy field. But now they were back. With their cameras ready. Sent down from heaven to save me from this scamming, toothless, money-grabbing fraudster.

'Oh, My Gawwwd!' Shrieked the female voice. 'A cow and a cute farmer in a hat! Jaaaake. Let's get a photo!'

The farmer's eyes darted. His head turned. New victims. Fresh blood. Richer-looking folk wearing light beige Birkenstocks. Fresh off the plane from a country where it is customary to tip. He stuffed my five dollar note into his deep trouser pocket and brushed past me.

Leading the beast towards his new customers.

We stayed in Hoi An for a month and cycled that road at least five more times. And each time we saw him. Walking slowly along on the same patch. The man in the triangle hat and his pet oxen. Smiling his toothy grin and waiting for silly women like me to stop.

So. My advice to you today is this.

If you are ever in Vietnam and happen to see a pumpkin man and a cow on a leash. For frigs sake, please. Keep pedalling.

It'll be good for your wallet and even better for your thighs.

Chapter Eight
Travel Trots

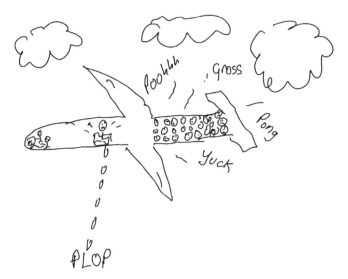

I got to be the ripe old age of thirty-nine before learning that the waste from aeroplane toilets is stored in a septic tank under the plane and emptied on arrival at the receiving airport.

Until then, I (honestly) believed that you weren't allowed to use the bathroom when the plane was stationary because the wee and poo would plop down that sucky shaft thing and be left sitting on the runway when the plane pulled away. Steaming.

Unlike the rest of my family, I managed to get through our entire time in South East Asia without a whiff of food poisoning.

'No Delhi belly for me,' I bragged when Sonny took to his bed for three weeks in India. 'My stomach is made of iron! Must be all those Yakults I drank in my twenties!'

And then, on an early morning flight from Vietnam to Hong Kong, aboard a plane carrying three hundred or so passengers, it happened. Quite suddenly and with no prior warning.

The travel trots.

It's not fair. Other travellers get ill from eating manky goat meat in Madagascar or mouldy yak cheese in Nepal. They come home and share heroic tales of when they were in Africa building a school and almost died drinking polluted water they'd sucked up through a paper straw.

In comparison, my story was a bit crap. Me? I ate some dodgy lettuce in Vietnam that had been washed in a bucket full of rank water. I can't even say it was fancy lettuce. It wasn't. It was just floppy and round. And contaminated.

Before we move on, let's talk about eating out in Vietnam. Just for a minute. Vietnamese cuisine is delicious, some of the best in the world. Fragrant, fresh, healthy, plentiful, it's gorgeous. To experience the true taste of Vietnam, I recommend you eat street food at one of the small local stalls. The ones with the doll-size plastic chairs outside.

But before you do, there's something you should know. Some advice you need to heed.

If you're in Vietnam and can't decide if an outside eatery is worthy of your Dong, here's a tip: look at how many used paper napkins are on the floor. You want to be aiming for at least fifty-eight. Why? Because only locals know to throw their dirty tissues on the ground when they've finished their meal, and locals don't eat in dodgy places. The more white tissues, the better the food.

I thought about this well-known piece of travel advice as I sat doubled over on the toilet of the Boeing 737. Speeding my way to Hong Kong with an arse full of explosive gas.

Twelve hours earlier, my family and I had wandered the streets of Da Nang. Hungry and tired. Grumpy because we had a 5 a.m. flight the next day, and we couldn't face getting up early. Unable to agree on a place to eat, we bickered and sulked. When the kids said they wanted to eat at the place that did burgers, I gave in. I couldn't be bothered arguing.

I should have known it was risky. There were no used napkins on the floor under the tables. Not one. I told myself this was because the owner was a clean freak who'd been out five minutes earlier and had cleared them away.

Silly me.

I didn't want to discuss my bowel movement with you in this book, but I have decided it's a must. Whenever I hear mention of a flight to Hong Kong, I smell diarrhoea. And I think it is only fair that you do, too.

Hands up.

What would you do if you were on a plane that was four minutes away from touch-down, and it suddenly became apparent that in approximately three and a half seconds, your bowels would open, and excrement would splurt everywhere, filling your seat (and most likely that of the person in front of you as well)?

Would you A: shit yourself and hope that no one notices?

Or B: ignore the seatbelt warning sign, leap out of your seat, run to the front of the plane where the hostess is strapped into her fold-down chair ready for landing, and blurt out, in your calmest voice, that you need the bathroom for a huge and urgent kak?

I'm glad you said B. You and I need to be friends.

I took off my seatbelt and made for the aisle.

'What are you doing, Mummy? What are you doing?' whispered Tessa, her voice in a heightened state of panic. She blocked my way with her knees.

My daughter hates flying. It terrifies her. She tells everyone we meet that it's her "phobia". Whenever we book seats for a flight, we have to ensure that she is sitting with Brian or me on one side and her brother on the other; otherwise, she starts hyperventilating and crying and showing us all up.

I have tried my hardest to help her through this blockage. Reassure her with my kindness. But all to no avail. No matter how often I tell her she has more chance of being burned alive in a horrific house fire than falling out of a tin box, flying really high above shark-infested water, and drowning, my words fail to console her.

'Can you please … move your legs ….,' I said between clenched teeth, terrified that if I opened my mouth too wide, the slimy goo would do a U-turn and exit through my face rather than my anus. 'I need … I need … Oh, TESSA! Just move your bloody legs so I can get through!' I barged past her knees, leaving her to watch helplessly as I shuffled along the row, clinging to the seats in front for support.

Guuurrgghh churned my stomach. *Oh, God. Any. Minute. Now.*

The stewardess didn't argue.

Either my white face told her I wasn't to be messed with, or she heard the warning signs emerging from my belly button—the hot steamy cauldron of Vietnamese salad sloshing around in stagnant water, ready to explode all over her navy blue starched A-line skirt.

'Be quick', she snapped before turning her fake red-lipsticked smile back to the passengers, who were now peering over the tops of the seats nervously, trying to decipher if a terrorist was on board and whether they should phone home and tell their partner about the money under the bed.

You don't need the details of what happened next; I'm sure you can imagine. All I will say is that when the plane wheels lowered onto the tarmac of Hong Kong International Airport, I was bent over double on the porcelain throne—squeezing and releasing—contracting and expanding. Sweating like a pig in a blanket. One of those silver lined emergency ones that get really hot.

Oink, oink, piggy, sweaty, oink, oink.

Brian has always dreamed of visiting Hong Kong. The Pearl of the Orient. Ever since watching Roger Moore in *The Man With The Golden Gun*, he'd talked of nothing else. If I'm honest, it was almost borderline freaky and obsessive.

When we first began dating, I would lay in his arms, and he would tell me stories of how Hong Kong was on loan to the British colony. Try and educate me. Kiss my head softly and promise that one day he would whisk me away to the city with the red pillar boxes and the twinkly harbour lights.

And now, here he was. In seat 22a of row G, his forehead pressed into the acrylic plane window looking out to the place of his dreams.

Unable to hold the hand of his wife because she was busy spraying the insides of the crapper with shite.

Don't believe anyone who tells you that the blue liquid that automatically fills the bowl of a plane toilet when you flush kills odours. It doesn't. They're lying. Or that aeroplane bathrooms carry spray air fresheners. They don't.

While you can find plenty of individually wrapped soap bars, mini toothbrushes and useless packets of grey polyester socks stashed away in the drawers under the sink, there is no sign, absolutely none, of a miniature Airwick spray.

With the urge to open and empty my wrenching bowel monetarily subsided, I stood in the tiny cubicle and faced the mirror. Shaking and drenched. Exhausted and clammy. Trying to psyche myself up to leave the safety of the room and walk back to my seat.

Urgh. I felt wretched.

My stomach was in knots. My backside was on fire. If it hadn't been for the fact that I knew my family were waiting for me, ready to disembark, I would happily have stayed in that little room for the rest of my life. Lived there. Died there. Just me and the toilet. Together forever, amen.

I put my ear to the door. Nothing. Just an eerie silence. The plane was stationary, but there was no sound or movement.

What were they doing out there? Why didn't they get up and leave? The captain must be waiting for something.

Oh my God, I hope it's not me....

Thoughts of a man in a hat sitting behind the wheel tapping at his watch and announcing to a plane full of passengers that he'll open the door just as soon as that woman comes out of the shitter flashed through my brain. I shook it away. *Stop it. Don't be stupid. He's probably in a queue on the runway. Either that or waiting for the crew to figure out where that monstrous stench is coming from.*

As inconspicuous as a woman who has just filled the plane with the smell of rotting guts can be, I opened the toilet door gingerly and stood in the aisle. The faces of three hundred passengers, each hovering over their seats like a bunch of eager greyhounds, shifted their eyes in my direction.

'How come she's allowed up?' boomed a voice from the back. It seemed they had forgotten about the terrorist in the lavvy.

Trolly Dolly's head spun to face me. 'Return to your seat quickly', she instructed, then she adjusted her hair grips and pressed her thumb into the side of her right nostril.

I took a step forward, ignoring the eyes that followed me. Whispering and pointing. Frowning and shuffling. My cheeks flushed. A rush of jittery uncertainty caused my feet to sweat. *Damn it. Where was I sitting? Which side was I on?* I scanned from left to right, searching for a familiar face in the crowd.

And then I saw her.

There. Shining like a beacon of light. Tessa. My thirteen-year-old daughter. Dripping in shame. Her mouth slightly open. Her eyes unnaturally wide. Flashing me a look that said, *don't you dare walk over here and sit next to me. DON'T. YOU. DARE.*

Wicked child. Horrid rat.

For all she knew, I could have been sucked down the toilet and spun into space—or even worse, trapped in the septic tank choking on a maternity sanitary pad.

I clenched my bottom and walked forward. Praying that I didn't have any stains on my trousers or toilet roll stuck to my shoe.

Row G. Thank God. I was safe.

I smiled frailly at my family. Tessa was holding the laminated safety card two inches from her face, intently studying every word. Sonny was pretending to be dead. I took my place next to Brian.

'Everything okay?' He said with eyes that were kind and concerned.

'Not really'.

I heaved out a long, dry sigh and blasted stale breath into his face. 'I'll tell you all about it later. Over dinner'.

He gave me a withered smile.

'Ding-dong'. The captain spoke.

'Ladies and gentlemen, welcome to Hong Kong. We are now ready to disembark. The skies are clear, and the temperature today is … clammy. Steamy. All over the place. Up and down like a whore's drawers. Sweating like a Glassblower's arse. Thank you for flying with Vietnam Airlines. We hope you enjoyed your flight'.

Chapter Nine

Japan

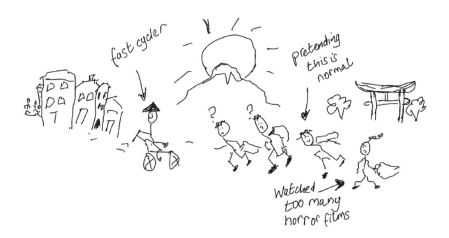

The Japanese people are probably the most considerate, polite, quiet and calm race of human beings I have ever encountered in my life.

After spending almost a month in this beautiful country, I felt as though I'd been on a meditation retreat. One with chilled vending machines stocked with cans of whisky and soda and delicious sandwiches. A retreat that provided toilets with heated seats and discreet tinkly music so no one hears you when you take a really long wee.

No matter how many books you read or films you watch, nothing can prepare you for Japan.

Like everyone else, I had preconceived ideas about the country nicknamed The Land of The Rising Sun. I thought it'd be mega expensive, with flying saucers hovering over neon skyscrapers and food portions so small and piddly that my family would be left writhing in hunger on the streets of Tokyo with nothing to eat but a piece of pink pickled ginger.

As it was, only one of these presumptions was correct—the expense.

Our visit to Japan was planned for May, coinciding with Golden Week, Japan's most important national holiday. I searched the internet for hours but failed to find decent accommodation for under three hundred dollars. And there was no way that was happening. Not on a budget of $100 a day.

Refusing to be beaten, I turned to an alternative way of seeing Japan. Couchsurfing. Sleeping in the houses of Japanese strangers for a month. For free.

The kids were horrified when I told them. 'Are you serious?' said Sonny. 'That's ridiculous! We don't even speak Japanese'.

He was right, of course. Our Japanese was non-existent. We spoke nothing. Not a word. Zilch. Not a single Nashi pear

What fun this would be.

Every person you meet in Japan is friendly and lovely, and kind. Don't believe anyone who tells you that the Japanese are cold-hearted warriors who want to stab you in the eye with a chopstick. It's not true.

My first encounter with a real-life Japanese person was by email. I reached out through the Couchsurfing website, requesting a place to stay. The man's reply was instant (and written in perfectly Googly-translated English). He said that he would be more than happy to accommodate us. That he was excited. He said he had two small children who would benefit hugely from learning English from my very intelligent and cooperative teenagers.

How kind.

I accepted enthusiastically, and the deal was sealed. Three nights of free authentic Japanese accommodation in exchange for a few measly English lessons from my sprogs.

Brilliant.

I didn't bother telling the kids about the tutoring arrangement. Not straight away. I thought it better to throw them in at the deep end once we arrived.

Two days before our stay, I spoke with the host on the telephone. We arranged a place and time to meet.

'You wait train station 5.10 p.m.', he barked down the phone in broken English.

'5.10', I repeated. 'Got it. Outside the railway station at 5.10. We'll be there'.

The day arrived, and, as agreed, we were outside Takamatsu train station at 4.55 p.m. Huddled together. Feeling anxious and apprehensive. Waiting to stay in the home of a Japanese stranger.

The mood was tense. My heart was pounding. This was not how I'd imagined the day to feel at all. As much as I hated to admit it, I was having second thoughts about what we were about to do. *What on earth was I thinking when I arranged this? How the hell would we communicate?*

The kids hated raw fish, and there was no way Brian's back would cope with sleeping on a hard floor.

Damn. I really wanted this Couchsurfing experience to be fun. For us all to feel excited.

I imagined being able to go home and brag to people about how we'd gone to the country with the most renowned language barrier in the world and managed to unite. English and Japanese. Two nations as one. Like those families you see on Facebook who take in millions of foreign foster kids during the summer break, and all become lifelong friends and end up marrying each other and having babies.

Why aren't we like that? Why can't we be open and trendy and get featured in the next Benetton campaign?

Pushing my doubts to one side, I attempted to lift the spirits. Gee, everyone up. Improve the groove.

'You know what they say!' I said brightly, ignoring Tessa's third complaint of nausea. 'Fear is excitement in disguise. So let's get to it, shall we? Let's turn those frowns upside down!'

(I wanted to add, cheer up you ungrateful little shits, but I didn't. Because that's not nice and not at all Benettony).

'Maaaann. I'm ab-so-lute-ly dreading this', groaned Sonny. He paced around the bags like a dog in a pound, wiping his hands down his thighs and looking to his sister for support. She jumped on the bandwagon.

'Me too. This is stupid. I feel sick. I'm going to throw up. Why can't you just tell the man that we've changed our minds and we'll book a hotel instead? I'll put my Christmas money towards it. I've still got that hundred dollars that Uncle Dave sent me. Can we? Pleeease?'

Christ. Parting with her own cash. She must be desperate.

The kids were right. This was ridiculous. In my unrealistic brain, I'd imagined cooperation and curiosity to come out of this Couchsurfing experience. Maybe a hint of deliriousness and 'mum-cred' at a push. Not dread and fear and quaking-in-our-boots terror. What had seemed like an out-there, exciting thing to do three weeks ago now seemed stupid and terrifying. In fifteen minutes, we were to be met by a Japanese stranger who would take us back to his Japanese house. For three nights.

Where we'd live.

Together.

In his house.

For thirty-six hours.

In Japan.

Oh, God.

'You're only doing this to look cool', said Sonny, slumping against a tiled wall in the corner of the railway station entrance. He slid to the floor and pulled his dirty rucksack between his knees. 'I thought you said we were coming to Japan to see that nuclear explosion place? Not stay with a bunch of strangers in a rubbish town'. He yanked at the zip of his bag and then threw his forehead dramatically into his hands.

Ungrateful Turd.

I smiled my nicest smile and shook my head forgivingly. Like a nursery school teacher on toilet duty whose kid has just slashed all over the floor, but she can't say anything because her job is to be patient and not to judge.

How wrong my young lad was.

The city of Takamatsu is built on the coast and smells of sea salt and warm tarmac. The pavements are so clean you can eat your dinner food from them. There is a lighthouse and shops and the most magnificent park you can imagine. Takamatsu is far from rubbish, thank you very much.

'There are loads of things to do here, actually', I chirped, desperate to lighten the mood before the Couchsurfing host arrived and realised that we were not the happy-go-lucky family that we claimed to be but rather a bunch of miserable bastards who just wanted a free place to stay in Golden Week. 'There's a huge mall with a McDonald's and everything'.

I waited. Sonny lifted his chin. I seized the moment.

'We could hire some bikes if you like. Tomorrow? Cycle out there for lunch?' *Liar.*

His eyes narrowed suspiciously. I watched as he pieced together memories in his brain. Too often, he'd been lured into a hot, sweaty bike ride with the end promise of an ice-cold treat, only to find said café closed and in its place a crappy little shack selling nothing but chewing gum and cigarette papers.

'I'll go', he said sullenly. 'But only if we can pre-order online before we leave'.

It was 5.02 p.m. The air was tense.

I looked at Brian. He was bent over, checking the straps on his backpack. Pulling them tight and then loosening them again. Standing up and tutting. Shaking his head. 'I knew I should have brought those bungee cords with me. These straps are a damn mess'.

Sometimes I suspect Brian has that OCDC thing. That disease where the victims believe nothing is ever right or good enough. Whenever he gets nervous or stressed, he cleans and fiddles. His backpack had been unloaded and re-sorted at least eighty nine times in the last three days. Underpants taken out and rolled that tiny bit tighter. Socks moved from one corner to the next. I watched as he stood up and brushed imaginary dirt from his knees, and I made a mental note to check our life insurance policy when we returned home. Everyone knows that people with brain disorders die early.

The digital clock above the ticket desk clicked, and the number furthest to the right changed to four. *It was nearly time.* I turned to Sonny.

'For God's sake', I hissed. 'I wish you'd put your bloody hood down. When the host turns up, he's going to think I've got a New York gangster for a son!' (Only I didn't say gangster; I said "gangsta" because that's how you talk to teenage boys). He turned away and pulled down hard on both sleeves. Great. Now he looked like a gangster with hacked-off hands.

My head was prickly. My feet were hot. All this to save a couple of hundred bucks a night. *What an idiot.*

I watched as people left the train station. Japanese men in expensive suits, striding cleanly. The heels of their leather shoes clicking on the concrete. Waving down Ubers, heading home to polish their Katanas and eat sushi.

5.07 p.m. Three minutes to go.

Brian offered me a weak smile. I looked away. *Not now, Brian.* I was mentally preparing myself. Wracking my brain for conversation topics. Something. Anything. Common-ground subjects to discuss over dinner with a Japanese family who didn't speak English.

What could we talk about? What do I know about Japan? Think Liz, think ….

Then it hit me.

Pearl Harbour. Of course! Just the thing! That'd show the Japanese family how well-informed we were. Who doesn't like to talk about boats and stuff?

5.09 p.m. The host showed up early. Breezing around the corner of the building on a bike. Like Fred from *Call the Midwife*, only thinner and with black hair and glasses. The first thing I noticed about him was how short his legs were. They were pint-sized; rather like a boy.

Of course, if I were a rude and insensitive woman who thought it hilarious and perfectly acceptable to laugh at other people's physical structure, I might have sniggered behind my hand and said, 'Ha-ha! Look at the man's little legs, kids! They only just reach the pedals! He reminds me of a little Oompa-Loompa'.

But I'm not, and I don't, so I didn't.

Anyway, everyone knows Oompa-Loompas aren't real. They were just a figment of Charlie's sugar-induced imagination.

I smiled like a ventriloquist. 'Stand up nicely', I said to the kids through clamped teeth. 'And don't you dare forget your manners'.

The bike pulled up alongside us, and the host dismounted.

Brian's shoulders squared and straightened. For a minute, I thought he might drop his pants and take his pecker out. Swing it around and do some kind of tribal dance. 'Me, tall English man. Me eat roast beef'. But he didn't. He smoothed his hair and smiled.

'Hello there', he said in an English accent that sounded more like a *Radio 4* presenter than my Scouse husband. 'I'm Brian'.

We all lined up in preparation. Waiting for our turn to greet the man.

'Hello', I blurted nervously. 'I'm Liz. Konnichiwa … Hello … Hi'.

Brian and the kids traded looks. They obviously didn't know that I'd watched the entire series of *Tenko* and could secretly speak Japanese.

The Couchsurfing man was kind and gentle. Gracious and patient. He placed his palms gently together and lowered his head and shoulders into a bow. 'Konnichiwa', he said, and we all returned the gesture. Unfortunately, I overcompensated and leaned too far forward, but luckily, Brian was next to me, and he grabbed the back of my shirt and pulled me back up.

Phew.

That could have been awkward. Ending my first-ever Japanese greeting ceremony with my nose mashed into the pavement.

I'll admit, I was shocked to have our host collect us on a bike. It's not the norm. Still, I decided to let it go. *This is Japan,* I told myself. *Everything's crazy cutting-edge here. I wouldn't be surprised if his bike hasn't got robotic powers.*

At 5.13 p.m., the spectacled Japanese man with short black hair and even shorter legs hopped back onto his bike and instructed us to follow him. 'House not far', he said rather unconvincingly and then pedalled off, leaving the four of us to follow. Jogging along the pavement behind him.

Oncoming pedestrians observed us curiously. Lowering their eyes respectfully before standing aside to let us pass. God knows what they must have thought. Four puffy Westerners hoofing it behind a man on a bike. Balancing their worldly goods in two packs—one on their backs, another on their fronts. Like a roll of pregnant armadillos parading down the street on their hind legs.

'Do you live far from here?' I shouted to the front of the line in the hope that the man might stop pedalling for a second and take pity on my beetroot cheeks and perspiring pits.

'You come'. Came the reply. From the back of his head.

I don't know much about much, but I know not to be fooled by a man riding a bike. Past experiences have taught me that you should never judge a person's wealth by what he drives or wears.

Back home in New Zealand, there was a farmer who used to own the land next to our house. He wore the same outfit every single day; a faded green cap, a tatty tee-shirt and a pair of shorts held together by twine. He would drive up and down the road, waving to us from the window of his clapped-out Ford Cortina.

One summer, the farmer invited us to his house for a BBQ. The four of us.

'That'd be nice', I said. 'Thank you, Farmer'.

I was half expecting a cup of warm milk served from a hay bale in the cowshed, but when we turned up at the address, I was gobsmacked. Behind two fancy wrought iron gates sat a sprawling mansion. A palace. A Kiwi hacienda. When the trickster farmer came to the door to greet us, he was smiling knowingly. Wearing a pale blue linen shirt that was clean and ironed, like a real-life grown-up. Unrecognisable from the tramp in the crusty Cortina.

Lying swine. I was glad when his farm got repossessed, and he went to live in Bennydale with his brother. Nobody wants a con man as a neighbour.

5.23 p.m. We had been trailing the pedalling Couchsurfing host through the streets of Takamatsu for ten minutes. Jogging at a speed of knots, passing houses big and small, tall and wide. Never stopping.

No conversation. No explanation.

'Mummy?' wheezed Tessa from behind. She reached out and pulled my shirt sleeve, almost causing me to topple sideways and break my ankle. 'Mummy … waaaiiit! Can you tell him to slow down? My Crocs are rubbing, and I want to ask you something!'

I turned to face her. Her cheeks were red and wobbly. She looked genuinely distressed.

'What? What is it? Quickly, hurry up. I don't want to get left behind'.

She bent over and began to pant.

'What if this…man…is…is…is a murderer?' she stammered, reaching down and scratching three lines into the soft skin of her foot. 'And he's… leading us to…to the old warehouse behind the station? I'm weirded out … I mean, how do you even know him? Hello? This is SO random and freaky'.

Idiotic child. She's obviously been watching too much Bates Motel on Netflix. Everyone knows there was only one mass murderer in Japan. And he was executed ten years ago.

I turned around and fell back in line. There was no way I was stopping. If I did, I wouldn't start again. To help keep me motivated (and to ward off a threatening stitch), I invented a game. I imagined I was a character from the Stephen King novel, *The Long Walk*. If I stopped, I'd be shot in the face, and everyone would witness me falling down dead. Splattered on the side of the road. With tire marks across my chest. I picked up the pace and inwardly congratulated myself on my clever imagery skills.

It's amazing what a positive mindset can do.

At last, the bike stopped. We were there. I looked around and squinted, gulping mouthfuls of air to fill my oxygen-starved lungs. We were standing on the pavement of a long street with traffic lights at either end and rows of shop fronts facing the road.

'Here my house', said the little man, gesturing over his shoulder, not even out of breath. His feet were on the floor, and his testicles were rammed into the crossbar.

And there it was. Just like that. A door. His front door. Discreetly wedged between two shops.

I blinked. Unable to decide if the entrance to his home was wonderfully secretive and intriguing, like something from Mr Benn, or terrifyingly dodgy and dangerous, like a holed-up heroin squat from *Trainspotting*.

Luckily it was the former.

As if by magic, the door to the man's house opened, and three people filed out onto the pavement to greet us. One, two, three. Pit, pat, pot.

The man's wife. Tiny and petite like a porcelain doll with shiny black hair and smooth pale skin. She smiled in my direction and bowed her dainty head. I thought about yanking her by the arm and asking if it was true that all Japanese women drank snake blood and smeared rice powder on their faces, but I decided now wasn't the time for girly talk. I'd save that for later.

I returned the bow and blinked like an owl.

Behind the man's wife were two small kids with freshly washed hair and jet-black eyes. A boy and a girl. Both unsmiling. Like Wednesday and Pugsley from *The Addams Family*. Standing like statues with their arms glued to their sides and their toes turned in.

I remembered the host's request on the telephone: 'Me, my wife, no English talk. The children from your children listen and learn the English'. *Shit. I'd forgotten about that.* I'd better tell Sonny to download Duolingo onto his phone.

With the introductions done and dusted, we entered the house through the little door and stepped into a narrow hallway. The man propped up his bike and turned to face us. 'Welcome my home', he said proudly. Waving his arms in all directions.

There were three white walls and a door. On one wall was a coat hook, and on the other two walls, there was nothing.

'It's lovely!' I gushed, trying to find something to look at.

'Yes, yes, really lovely'. 'This is very nice'. 'So cool', Brian and the kids chimed in unison.

I looked around. This was a narrow teeny-tiny house. Rather like the one that they used in the film *Stuart Little*. A small Japanese house made for tiny Japanese mice.

Usually, when you enter a stranger's home (especially one where you'll be staying for the next three nights), the owners give you a quick tour. Show you around. We waited. And waited. The eight of us packed like sardines in the confined hallway. The boy and girl lurked behind their mother's legs. The rest of us stood opposite each other. Smiling.

I touched the wheel of the bike. The man nodded and smiled. I smiled back. Brian gestured to the coat hook and smiled. The woman shrugged her shoulders as if to say, 'It's just a coat hook' and then smiled. We all smiled together. My jaw began to ache.

To break the ice, I decided to turn my attention to the little children. I'm good with kids—even weird ones. I was one myself years ago.

'And what are y---o---u---r n---a---m---e---s?' I asked, sounding like an elephant with facial paralysis.

Their mother reached for the children's hands and gently coaxed them out from behind her legs.

'They name Hinata and Emiko'. She smiled proudly.

The children giggled and shook their mop of dark hair and then opened their mouths to reveal two rows of sharp little milk teeth fangs.

Yikes.

I tilted my head to the side. The way you do when you go to a modern art exhibition and don't have a clue what you're looking at. 'Awww. Cute', I said and then started to laugh nervously because I couldn't think of anything else to say.

Brian came to my rescue. He knelt before the pair and wiggled his fingers under the little boy's chin. 'When my son was your age', he teased playfully, 'he used to have a little friend ... and HE was called the TICKLE MONSTER!! Grrrrr!!'

Ignoring the look of terror spreading rapidly across the child's face, he ran his fingers across the boy's puny shoulders, then grabbed at his own throat and pretended to fall and choke. 'Aarrgggg! Saaave mee!!'

Fuck me, no. You have to be kidding me.

The hallway fell silent.

Sonny touched the valve cap on the bike tyre. My toes clawed at the soles of my shoes.

The kid stared at Brian in disbelief. His eyes wide with fear, his chest heaving. Petrified. The wife was visibly shaken. She covered her mouth and let out a small cry. Surely her husband hadn't invited a pedo into her Japanese home built for tiny mice?

'You come', said the man quickly, and we began our ascent up a flight of narrow stairs, heaving our heavy bags behind us.

The living quarters of the small but tall house were on the first floor. We were shown to our room by the host and his wife, who promptly disappeared to the kitchen down the hall, leaving us to unpack.

The space was tight and had no windows. Still, four freshly made futons were arranged on the floor in a square, and a makeshift curtain of transparent material had been draped across the doorway to offer temporary privacy. This would do nicely. More than we could ask for.

I plonked my bag on the skinny mattress and rubbed my neck. We'd only been here for twenty minutes, and already I was knackered. *What I wouldn't give for a glass of wine. Or a large gin and tonic. I'd even take a bottle of warm baby milk on the hay bale from the farmer if it meant I could lay down and close my eyes.*

When you are a Couchsurfing guest, regardless of whether you've travelled all day on a train and you're hungry and tired and don't want to make conversation with two mini vampire children, your role is to help out. Mingle. Be part of the family.

You do not treat the place like a hotel.

'Unpack what you need, and then let's go and socialise', I said with a tone of enthusiasm that I hoped sounded convincing. I smoothed down the clean sheets longingly. Making a mental note of how many hours it would be before I could lay under them.

I was just about to round everyone up and leave the room when all of a sudden, I heard something.

'He-he-he! Ssshhhh'.

Voices. From behind the curtain. Small voices. A rustle and a push. *They were back. The kids. Standing on this side of our privacy. In our room. Peering at us. Staring. In Japanese.*

The tickle monster obviously hadn't deterred them. Either that or they had bionic self-refreshing memory banks that ran on futuristic rechargeable batteries.

'Hello again!' I said pleasantly, trying to remind myself that I was a mother and liked children because why else why would I be taking two of them around the world? But it didn't work. I hated them. I wanted to kill them. 'Have you come to join us?'

Zilch. No flicker of life. Devoid of emotion.

This was going to be a long three days.

I cocked my head and listened out for their parents. Silence. *Hmm, I knew their game.* I bet they'd fled and sent the two offspring along the corridor to receive their first English lesson. Decided to take advantage of the built-in babysitting service. I wouldn't be surprised if, right now, they weren't riding their bike through the streets of Takamatsu. Him on the front, her on the back. Rejoicing their freedom. Riding along with no hands, singing the Japanese national anthem at the top of their voices. Naked.

I scanned the neat but minuscule room. Brian was unpacking his flight bag and laying out the necessary charging cables he needed to use that night. Sonny was searching for Wi-Fi. Tessa stood facing the two children in the entranceway. Glued to the spot.

'What are they doing?' she whispered in a voice that was far too loud to use in a house with walls made from paper. 'Why are they so … weird?'

If I could have, I would have gagged her with a pillowcase and sat on her head.

'Tessa!' I scolded, flashing an apologetic smile towards the children. No need. Not a flicker. Just the same vacant stares.

'They remind me of those two dead kids from *The Shining*. The ones who hung around the corridors watching that kid whizz up and down on his bike'.

Gulp.

My mind went downstairs to the bike in the hallway.

Surely not?

My daughter raised her arm slowly, like a marionette. The children's eyes followed her every movement. Mesmerised. Unblinking. Like those Action Man Eagle Eye dolls that were all the rage in the 1970s.

This was ridiculous.

Recalling the deal I made with their father, I picked up Brian's bag from the floor and pointed to it, smiling at the youngsters whose names I had forgotten.

'B-aa-gg', I said, rattling the strap and mouthing the word to help them along. Six years of homeschooling has taught me all there is to know about teaching. Slow and loud. That's the trick.

Nothing. Null and void. I swallowed and was about to try again when I noticed the little girl's eyes darting to something behind me.

'Can you not? Get OFF me!!'

It was Tessa. Wailing in her fake American accent. Arguing with her brother over the sleeping arrangements. Straddling a mattress like a possessive witch. Claiming ownership of the neatly made futon beneath her while hurling punches at Sonny, who was taunting her, flailing his lanky arms in front of her face.

'This is MY place. I was here first. Get away from my pillow with your dirty feet, you stupid filthy PIG!' she screeched like a spoiled brat.

Nice, Tess. Nice.

I turned to the doorway in a panic. Praying that the kids had left. Shit. No. They were still there. Clocking every word with their supersonic Japanese computer-like brains. Ready to repeat to Papa what they had learned in their first English lesson.

I held my breath. The duo faced each other. Slowly and in perfect English, they repeated what they had heard.

'Stew-pid-fill-theey-peeg'. Again. Just so it stuck. 'Stew-pid-fill-theey-pig'.

The host came out of the kitchen and called us for dinner. The curtain flickered.

And as if by magic, the children were gone.

Chapter Ten
Venice

If you go to Italy, try and fly in and out of Venice Marco Polo. For some reason, this airport has the cheapest flights. People tend to go to Rome or Milan, but take it from me, if you want to save money, fly to Venice and begin your Italian adventure from there.

You might imagine Venice airport to be filled with canals. I know I did. I thought the aeroplanes would have big rubber jet skis that lowered down onto the water and that all the passengers and their bags would be chucked into the Grand Canal. Screaming. Left to fend for themselves. Flapping around helplessly in the murky Venetian waters while those from first class flagged down all the gondolas.

But no.

Marco Polo Airport is located on the mainland. It is approximately a thirty-minute drive from the centre of Venice. And it is very, very dry.

A month before arriving in Italy, while we were still in Japan, I had spent hours on the internet looking for cheap places to stay in Venice. Not easy when you're on a tight budget. I'd even tried to find a Couchsurfing host, but it seemed that no families lived in Venice. Not ones that wanted to offer their spare bed to a family of four scabbers at least.

So an Airbnb it was.

I eventually found a place on the outskirts of Venice which was bang on budget. A room in an apartment with a diddy shared bathroom and an even diddier communal kitchen. Hardly the Italian dream but hey, for fifty dollars a night, who cares?

Pack your bags, bambinos; Mama's taking you to Italy.

'Can we see the pictures?' the kids asked when I told them we'd be staying in a legit paid-for place and not on the floor of someone's house for free.

'There aren't any', I lied.

The Airbnb photos were crap. There was no way I was sharing them. I wasn't in the mood to listen to Tessa telling me (once again) about how her best friend went to Venice and stayed in a hotel with pink velvet curtains and a fish tank in the bathroom.

We hired a car from Venice airport and drove to the Airbnb located about twenty minutes away in a small town with a name I can't recall. I do know that it sounded similar to Doz or Dos because

Sonny made some cocky-arse comment about the name having negative connotations.

'I hope this town isn't a doss hole', he joked, smirking sideways at his sister. I tutted and pushed my seat back, forcing his knees a little closer to his chest.

No one likes a smarty-pants.

Whenever we drive to somewhere we haven't stayed before, the same thing happens. Five minutes before our arrival, the kids start to get nervous. Twitchy. Worried about where they'll be sleeping. They watch the satnav like hawks. Fix their eyes on the little blue flag that represents the final destination and then hold their breath. *I know. Freaky.* Not until we get to where we're going do they relax and suck in air again.

Sometimes I worry that this trip has traumatised them. Paved the way for some very serious breathing defects later in life. Surely it's not normal for children to deprive their lungs of oxygen for so long while sitting in the back of a car?

*Side note: after writing this, I Googled: "what is the longest time a mammal has ever held its breath" and found out that it's the Cuvier's Beaked Whale. Apparently, those things can go without breathing for almost four hours. Phew. I feel much better now. This means that I can stop asking the kids if their chests hurt every time they sneeze.

As we drove along the Italian roads, passing shambly romantic villas painted dusky pink and eggshell blue, the kids pressed their noses to the window. Longingly. The car indicator clicked down, and we turned left into a 1970s shitty-looking square-shaped precinct. A cross between a council-run retirement village and one of those car parks where druggies go to deal smack. A handful of low-rise apartments sat above a launderette, a lottery shop, a dog grooming salon, and a pizzeria.

The kids groaned and threw their heads into the back of their seats. 'Oh, God … Pleeease … No'.

'There's our one!' I pointed up to the scummy building with the painted number 12 splashed across the dirty grey pebbledash. The apartment was above the pizzeria.

Lovely. Very Italian.

Ignoring the negative tension in the car, I commended myself on this rare find. *Well done, me!* Things weren't so bad after all; I'd rather lay in bed smelling hot salami all night than wet dog fur.

As luck would have it, the pizzeria was open, and the smell of melted cheese and fresh oregano softened the disappointment that this was our first night in Italy and we were staying in a hideous concrete bunker at the back of a housing estate.

'Guess what we're having for tea?!' I piped, using my I-know-this-is-really-crap-but-let's-pretend-otherwise voice. (What I *really* wanted to say was, 'Cheer up, you ungrateful, moaning, sour-faced little gits'. But I didn't. Because I'm nice.)

'Pizza! Hurray! You can even have extra pineapple if you behave yourselves and smile'.

The Airbnb lady met us at the door with an excessive amount of enthusiasm. 'Welcaamm! Cam in!' she oozed, throwing her arms into the air and almost smashing the low-hanging glass lampshade across the bridge of Sonny's nose.

Blimey. Fifty dollars must buy you a lot in Italy.

She didn't look at all Italian. Not one bit. Aside from her sexy accent, I would have pegged her as Nordic. Or Icelandic. Or Scotch. She had pale freckly skin and orange hair. Like Tilda Swinton but without the pointy ears.

Brian's shoulders slumped with disappointment.

We smiled and followed her through the narrow hallway into a tiny enclosure with just enough space to fit a double bed and a set of bunks. Huddling together in the centre of the room. All four of us on one tile. 'Theees is your ruuume!' beamed Tilda. 'Enjoy eet!'

Christ. We've stayed in some small places, but this took some beating. I'd hired bigger skips for less money.

My mind flashed to that scene in the film *Titanic.* The one where the Irish family with all the screaming kids open the door and squeeze on top of each other into the third-class cabin. I blinked. Sometimes I wish I was American. Then I'd be brave enough to say how I really felt. But I'm not. So I didn't.

'Oh, look at this … This is adorable! I love it! This is perfect. Thank you so much'.

Tessa flashed me a look. The look that kids give their mothers when they hate them and want to file for a separation order. I ignored her. My attention was on Sonny, who was pulling back the flimsy blind with his huge, clumsy shovel hands in an attempt to open the window.

'It's stack'. Tilda offered an indifferent shrug. 'Sarrrry huh?'

'Not to worry', I panted, wiping the moisture across my eyebrows and wishing I'd used Tessa's deodorant and not that natural rubbish stuff that smelled of geranium oil and sweat. 'We've slept in hotter places than this. Haven't we, kids?' I was going to start naming a few, but I couldn't think of one, so I just smiled instead.

We exited the room in single file. Shuffling so as not to step on the heel of the person in front. Tessa gripped my elbow. 'Mummy!' she whispered dramatically. 'We're here for three nights. You *know* what Sonny's like when he doesn't have a fan. Do you think we'll even be able to sleep?'

I dug my nails into my moist palm and took a sharp breath in.

If I was the sort of mother who didn't care about her daughter's feelings, I might have said. 'What do you think, MORON? We are staying in an apartment above a pizzeria. Sleeping in a bedroom that sits on top of a woodfire oven. There is no air conditioning. Or fan. The window doesn't open, and to top it all, your mother is in the middle of perimenopause, dealing with a body temperature that flashes between boiling point and MILDLY ROASTING. So NO. In answer to your question, *sweetness*, we will NOT be sleeping. Not for at least THREE FUCKING NIGHTS'.

But I'm not. And I do. So I didn't.

'Of course, we'll sleep, darling, don't you worry about that', I said, like a normal parent and not one with split personality issues. 'Everyone knows that Italy gets chilly at night. It'll be fine, you'll see'.

I swished her ponytail reassuringly and felt my nose grow an inch or two.

It's hard when you are staying in a shared Airbnb. Especially one so small. You never know where to go or what to do with yourself.

The kids found a plug by the kitchen table and hooked themselves up to the internet drip. Staring at their screens like a pair of addicts. Brian did that thing he always does when he feels awkward and is at a loss about what to do next. He went to the toilet. With his phone.

I hadn't realised that the apartment would be quite so small. There was no room to swing a hamster, let alone a dead cat. The two bedroom doors almost touched; they were that close. The lounge had one black leather sofa, a flat-screen TV and lots of Italian DVDs scattered all over the floor.

Our host was kind. 'You can watch teevvveey if you are wanting'. There was a moment of uncomfortable silence. I couldn't think of anything more torturous than sitting in this baking hot, minuscule flat watching telly with Brian, an Italian elf, and two miserable kids.

Sod that. No way. Forget it.

'Thank you', I said, running my fingers lightly across the plastic DVD cases. 'That's a brilliant idea. We might watch a film later on'. Tessa looked up from the kitchen table. A flicker of hope ran from one eyebrow to the other. 'Maybe after the children have done some research on what there is to do in Venice'.

When I was a little girl, I would visit my grandma in Lancashire. My grandma had lots of friends. Her house was the go-to place on the street. Because I was my grandma's favourite and my mum wasn't there to tell me off, rather than play outside in the fresh air, I'd spend my days in the back room, listening to adult conversations. Rocking away on the rocking chair. Breathing in masses of second-hand Woodbine smoke and wondering what the word hysterectomy meant.

My grandma wasn't keen on everyone who came to call. Take Edna, the woman from the cul-de-sac across the road. Whenever Edna popped in for a brew and dared ask my grandma for more milk or made a comment about the price of stockings, my grandma would wait for her to leave, then she'd turn to me and say, 'Ohhh. I don't

know what's got into that Edna lately. She's acting all manic. Mytherin'
me with her manic-ness. She meks me sweat cobbs that Edna'.

I never forgot that word. Manic. I knew exactly what it meant.
Manic.

Someone who isn't quite right. Like Edna.

The host was called Micha. She was lovely. But … I don't know.
Something was off. I could feel it in my ovaries. She talked far too
quickly and was far too excitable for my liking. She was manic.

She was in her bedroom with the door closed. I could hear her
laughing and joking and talking rapidly in Italian. I wanted to take one
of the chairs from the kitchen and force it under the door handle so
she couldn't get out and had to stay there all night. But I didn't. The
last thing I needed was a bad review from Airbnb.

The toilet flushed, and Brian emerged sheepishly from the
bathroom. Slipping his phone back into his pocket. *Gross*. I'd talk to
him later about how I felt about the phone and toilet thing, but for
now, there was a more urgent matter that needed discussing. I grabbed
him by the shoulder and pulled him into the sweatbox bedroom.

'What's going on?' he said, straightening his polyester shorts.

'Her', I mouthed, jerking my thumb towards her closed bedroom
door. 'The host. *Micha*. She's a bit weird, isn't she? What's with all the
hyper-laughing? Why does she never sit still? Something doesn't feel
right. She reminds me of that woman in that film, the one with the
obsessive flatmate'.

Nice Liz. Super friendly.

Brian looked at me and frowned, and I instantly regretted sharing
my thoughts with him. He had desperately wanted our first night back
in Italy to be a special experience. He'd even suggested that we fork

out for a nice hotel next to a small romantic canal. But no. Here he was. In el budgito. Sweating like a sow in a sauna. Listening to his paranoid wife bad-mouthing someone just because they had orange hair and smiled a lot.

Sulkily, I sat down on the bed.

The trouble with him was that he was so busy being Mr Nice-Guy that he didn't realise when something was amiss. 'Forget it', I huffed, slapping my hands on my knees like old men do when they've been waiting for ages at the doctor's surgery and their name is finally called. 'Just don't blame me if we're all slaughtered in our beds'. He turned to leave. 'And stop taking your phone to the toilet. It's bloody disgusting'.

Later that night, we ate pizza together. The five of us. It seemed rude not to ask Micha to join us. What with her living there and practically sitting on our laps when we were all in the same room.

Back in New Zealand, I had dreamed of this day. Our first night in Italy. Eating pizza with my darling children. Sharing the tale of when Brian asked me to marry him in Verona. Drinking red wine and laughing jovially like one of those trendy bohemian families who swear and don't care.

But the reality was very different.

Four hot and sweaty bodies, knackered and cranky. Choking down pizza that didn't have enough cheese. Trying to figure out how to say "pedestal fan" in Italian.

'This is lovely pizza ….' I babbled like a sag-winged bat. 'At home, we make our own pizza, don't we, Sonny? But it's not as nice as this … Mmmm … This is delicious … I don't know what it is about mozzarella in Italy …. It's so stringy and tasty, and … there's always plenty of it ….' My words trailed off. No one was listening.

After dinner, I sent the kids down to the recycle bins in the car park to dispose of the cardboard boxes. 'If anyone asks you your name or offers you any sweets that look like tablets, make sure you say no and run straight home', I warned.

Sonny slammed the apartment door on his way out.

With the kids out of the way and Brian fiddling with something electronic in the bedroom, Micha and I began to bond. She even offered to share some of the local hot spots with me.

'You masst go to the book shap in Venice. Is famous for having many, many cats. It is very buuutiful. You like that I show you on map?'

Relieved that I wouldn't have to stay up all night Googling *"cool and undiscovered places to visit in Venice"* to impress the kids the next day, I accepted her offer gladly. I sat on the couch with my hands on my lap, so she had room to sit down.

How kind.

Maybe she wasn't a psychopath after all.

Taking a pen and a piece of paper from the glass shelf beside the TV, Micha scribbled down instructions on where we were to catch the train and how to find the kitty bookshop. And then, quite abruptly and with no warning, her mood changed. She claimed to have a headache and went off to bed.

Hmmm. My suspicions returned. I thought of Edna.

When you are staying in an Airbnb with two bedrooms joined at the hip, a tiny kitchen, a telly that only broadcasts in Italian, and a host who goes to bed with a headache, you go to bed, too. I climbed into the sticky sheets, whispering my concerns to the kids about the Scottish-Italian landlady.

'Well, I think she's *really* nice', said Tessa, rolling over in the bottom bunk and pummelling the pillow with her fist. 'Honestly, Mummy, you're sooo judgemental. Why can't you just let people be?'

Christ. That's a bit rich coming from her.

I was about to remind the little madam of how she'd laughed hysterically at a woman in the airport yesterday. The one in the wig. But I didn't. Every good parent knows you don't sweat the small stuff. I lay sideways and thrust my backside into Brian's belly to increase his body temperature. There. That'll teach him to check the Liverpool scores instead of paying attention to my female intuitions.

The next morning, we were up and out of the apartment before Micha came out of her room.

We took the train to Venice and spent the next six glorious hours wandering along beautiful narrow lanes and crossing ornate bridges. Taking photographs of pigeons and men in red and white stripy tops who strutted up and down on big, long throbbing gondolas.

In the afternoon, I suggested we be like a real Italian family and bathe our feet in the water. I took off my shoes and dipped my toes into the canal. Laughing coyly like a halfwit. Pretending that I was doing something daring and that the lukewarm water had taken my breath away.

'Are you sure you should be doing that?' said Tessa, frowning and staring into the depths. 'It looks pretty gross to me. Why is it all brown? And anyway … Becky Boyd's mum said it's illegal for tourists to put their feet in the canal in Venice'.

I wanted to say: 'That's because Becky Boyd's mum is a crabby-arsed Bible basher who never likes my posts on Facebook'.

But I didn't.

Because I'm mature, and sometimes I wear my glittery cross like Madonna. I pulled my baggy pants up over my knees and thought of Joanna Lumley: 'We're travellers, darling, not tourists. There's a big difference'.

On the other side of the canal, a beautiful couple was also indulging in some toe-dipping. A man and a woman. Lovers. Giggling and touching. Flirting with each other like I don't know what. I fixed my eyes on the oblivious pair, then shifted the weight on my bum cheeks so I could get comfy. Touch, touch, touch. Kiss, kiss, kiss. Jesus Christ. *Get a room.* Anyone would think that they were in the most romantic city in the world or something.

Sonny was talking to me, but I ignored him. I was too busy making up a story about Romeo and Juliet over there on the other side of the canal.

I bet they were married. To different people. And they were meeting up in secret to cheat on their partners. *Yes. That was it ….. They'd agreed to meet in Venice. To have dirty illicit sex.* The woman raised her chocolate brown eyes to meet mine. *Shit.* I flushed and looked away. I didn't want her to think I was spying on her. Gawping. Perving. I waited for a second or two before sneaking another look. She giggled breezily and draped herself over the man's shoulder seductively. Nibbled flirtatiously on his earlobe like a black-haired dormouse.

Crikey.

I watched. Gormlessly. Unashamedly transfixed. The man tossed his head back playfully, and then, 'Ah-wooooooooooo', he pretended to howl.

The spell was broken.

Oh my God …. Urgh. What a pair of show-offs. I picked at the flaky dead skin on my right kneecap.

Maybe they were one of those exhibitionist-type couples who liked to be watched. *Swingers. Nymphomaniacs. I'd heard about their sort before.* Brian's old mate from work used to know a couple who went to Asda's car park every Saturday night to have sex in the back of their Ford Mondeo. They were at it for months. Paying and displaying until they were told to move on.

I looked at Brian sitting next to me. Examining his veiny foot. Rotating his ankle around in a clockwise motion and flinching and tutting every time it clicked.

Yuck.

If he tells me one more time how his foot has never recovered from that tennis injury, I'll throw him under the next gondola.

Venice is beautiful, but it's busy. And hot. The four of us decided we would spend the next day relaxing. Driving along Italian roads with our air conditioning on full blast. This is the kids' favourite thing to do in the world; It means that they get to listen to their *Harry Potter* talking book with their dad instead of being forced to pay attention to their mother-cum-teacher rabbiting on about how the roads in Italy are long and straight because the Romans built roads to last and were very good fighters, too.

Next morning. 7.40 a.m. In the bathroom with Brian

When a family of four stays in an Airbnb with only one bathroom and are trying their hardest to get out early, it is best that the parents go into the bathroom together. To save on time.

Brian was squinting into the fogged-up mirror, trying to shave over the tiny yellow sink, and I was behind the shower curtain with my face held up to the sprinkler. Pretending to be Janet Leigh in *Psycho*.

Knock, knock, knock on the bathroom door.

Damn. I'd woken Micha. 'Won't be a minute!' I called in my best polite voice.

The knock came again. Louder this time. 'Mummy. Can you come out here for a minute?'

My knees and nipples bristled in unison—those little shits. I had *told* them to be quiet so as not to wake Micha. They *knew* I wanted to get on the road early. My last instruction to them as I heaved myself out of bed and into the bathroom this morning was to 'BE QUIET'. The last thing I wanted to do was spend an hour making polite conversation about some stupid flea-ridden cats in a boring bookshop.

Crossly, I threw one leg over the slippery bath and reached for a towel.

This had better be important.

I opened the door forcefully to show my children that I meant business. 'Whaa—' I took a sharp breath in. Stopped in my tracks. Shocked by what I saw.

There was Micha. The host. Dressed in her shorts and tee-shirt. Standing two inches from my face. Sonny and Tessa behind her. Quivering. Their faces as white as ghosts. Panic-stricken.

'Ermmm … she doesn't know who we are'. Sonny. Looking like a five-year-old child. 'She is saying that we are trespassing'.

What the? That cheeky Manky Miss. I couldn't believe my ears.

I don't know if this has ever happened to you, but you know when something so bizarre happens, and it happens so quickly that your brain doesn't have time to catch up? So you tell yourself that what is happening isn't actually real … and then you feel as though you have floated out of your body and are watching everything unfold in front of you like a film. Have you ever felt like that? **Please say yes. You'll make me feel like a total nut-case who obviously needs some sort of exorcism treatment if you say no.*

At first, I thought it was some sort of joke.

A trick the kids had planned to make me look stupid. 'Hey, Micha. Watch how red my mum's face is when she gets out of the shower, and we tell her that her fears of you being a psychopath were correct all along'.

But this was no joke. The woman who, twelve hours earlier, had welcomed us into her home and had eaten pizza with me on the couch now looked at me as if for the first time.

'Who are you? Why are you in my house?' Her voice was both angry and confused. Forceful but fragile.

I swallowed. Water dripping from my elbows.

'It's me, Micha. It's Liz'. Not a flicker of recognition. No sign of a joke.

'I want you to get out of my house. Now'.

Shit.

'I'll be right out', I muttered. Confused. 'Just let me get dressed'.

Looking back, I can't believe that I shut the bathroom door and left the kids alone with her. For all I knew, she could have been away with the fairies. Doolally. Imagine the Italian headline: 'Kids Slain in Beds by Mad Scottish Italian Impersonator While Mother Fiddles Getting Wet Tits into Bra'.

Micha was standing in the kitchen when we came out of the bathroom. Her arms folded defiantly across her body. Her chin held upwards. Waiting for an explanation as to why the hell we were in her apartment. I didn't know what to do. My first thought was to call someone. The Airbnb website, maybe? *No. That won't work.* You make your booking through the website, but all correspondence is between the host and the guest.

I wanted to talk to her. For her to recognise me and stop fucking around. I stood in the doorway of the kitchen and spoke softly.

'We are the family staying with you. We arrived yesterday, on Wednesday. Remember?'

No. She was having none of it.

'Let's just go, Mummy ....' pleaded Tessa, who was hiding in the bedroom on the bottom bunk.

'Just call the police!' said Sonny, strutting between the bedpost and the window that didn't open.

Brian and I had no idea what to do. Here we were in a country where we couldn't speak the language in an apartment with a woman who could have flipped at any time, claiming we were trespassing in her home.

And $50 a night I had paid for this. *What a con.*

And then I remembered. The piece of paper that Micha had used to write train schedules and the map detailing where we could find the cat book shop.

I went to my flight bag and pulled out the note. There it was. I had it. The evidence that proved we were there the night before. I walked back into the kitchen. Like Miss Marple about to reveal the vicar.

I remember thinking how strange everything felt. There was no noise in the apartment. No kettle boiling, no toaster toasting. No TV. Just an eerie sense of calm. That feeling of trepidation when something is about to go one way or the other.

I approached slowly. Cagily. 'Here', I said, gently putting the piece of paper into Micha's hand. 'You wrote this out for me yesterday. Remember?'

Her eyes scanned the note. A look of helplessness flooded her face. She stared at the words for what seemed like hours and then blinked back tears. She said nothing. Looked at no one. Clutching the note, she turned and went to her bedroom.

Seconds later, she reappeared with her phone and a small black notebook filled with lots of phone numbers. She stood in front of me with her hands trembling. She found a page and dialled. Tears rolled down her cheeks. After three rings, she spoke rapidly in Italian.

I wanted so much to take her in my arms and comfort her. Ease her confusion. Every motherly instinct told me to take her and hold her tight. Reassure her. But I didn't want to frighten her. To her, I was a stranger, and I was afraid of invading her space and alarming her.

Ten minutes later, an ambulance pulled up outside, followed by a smartly dressed man in a small black Fiat Punto. They parked haphazardly and climbed the stairs, opening the door without knocking. They went straight to Micha. Comforting, controlling, using reassuring voices that were hushed and low. The woman paramedic brushed Micha's hair back from her tear-stained face and wrapped a soft grey blanket around her quivering shoulders while the doctor gently asked questions and took notes.

And all the while, the four of us stood in the apartment. Taking up space. Unsure of what to do next. Not knowing what to say to three Italian health professionals who hadn't yet asked how we were related to this patient and why we were in her apartment.

Within ten minutes, Micha was ushered downstairs by the paramedics.

She didn't say goodbye. Gave no explanation, no contact number, no key. She just left. Guided firmly by the elbow into the waiting ambulance.

It was the doctor who stayed behind and explained everything to us.

Using broken English, he told us that Micha was on medication for a severe condition. If she missed any medication, it affected her memory and put her in danger. She had rented her room out as a way to meet people. To live life as fully as possible. But unfortunately, she had forgotten (or chosen not to) take her medication.

We packed our bags and left the apartment. The car remained silent for the next two hours.

Six weeks later

After spending time in Croatia and Montenegro, we returned to Italy. We were heading South to visit Pompeii, but before making the drive, we went somewhere else. To Venice. And we spent the night with Micha.

I'm not sure why, but in an odd kind of way, I felt connected to her. Like she was our responsibility. We had only known this girl for twenty-four hours, but I felt protective towards her, and I wanted her to know that we were her friends. That we were fine with what had happened.

Plus, she still owed us $100 for the two unused nights.

The evening was lovely. We sat together eating pizza, and she laughed as we shared stories about the funny things that had happened to us in Croatia. Nobody mentioned what had happened six weeks earlier. It was forgotten.

The next day, when we awoke, Micha had gone. She was meeting friends to go swimming and had left early. We had been given instructions on where to leave the key. On the kitchen table was a note written on the back of a paper napkin.

It said this:

Dear family, it gives me hope and makes my heart sing with happiness to know that these are people like you in the world. Keep travelling and keep being you. I'm sorry if I cause the nuisance.

Micha x

CHAPTER ELEVEN
MONTENEGRO

Montenegro is every bit as beautiful as people say it is. Orange-roofed houses butt against steep green hills stretching from the sky to the Adriatic Sea below. White fishing buoys bob lazily in the crystal clear water, and shingle beaches merge with narrow twisty roads offering tantalising views with each turn. Random clusters of wild hollyhocks stand at attention along the roadside—their delicate pink colour a stark contrast to the gloomy green mountains beyond.

But not everything in Montenegro is rosy and flowery.

There are some things I would happily pay to forget...

We visited Montenegro in June. The month of Tessa's birthday. My daughter was super excited to spend her fourteenth birthday in Europe and talked of nothing else prior.

'I can't believe it!' she gushed to her brother, who was set to be spending his birthday later that month in a remote farming hamlet in Croatia, 'I get to celebrate my big day in one of the swankiest European resorts in the world! This is going to be the BEST birthday ever. I bet I'll NEVER forget this birthday!'

Our Montenegrin Airbnb was set high in the hills. It was nothing fancy, but it was comfortable. And cheap.

It had one large bedroom with a double bed for Brian and me, a single for Tessa, and a small adjoining lounge/kitchen with a small wooden dining set and a couch that turned into a bed for Sonny. He moaned when he saw it and said he wouldn't be able to sleep because of the smell of cooking fat. I suggested he rub some of his dad's Tiger Balm around the inside of his nostrils.

It's true. My maternal kindness has no limit.

Compared to the rest of the apartment, the bathroom was quite posh. A bit chavvy but nice all the same. It had mock marble tiles on the floor, gold-plated bath taps, and that glittery grouting you'd sometimes see in the ladies toilets of 1980s nightclubs. The owners had obviously worked on this room first and run out of money when the time came to buy white goods. The cooker and fridge looked like they'd rolled out of Steptoe's yard.

Outside the apartment, past a shared washing line, was a BBQ. It wasn't the most sophisticated of set-ups. It looked like something Ickle Pickle had thrown together with clay; nevertheless, it was provided for our use. And it was free.

The day before her birthday, Tessa buzzed with excitement. She talked of trips to the city, meals at restaurants and repeatedly Googled the price of pink Converse boots.

'Let's have something special for dinner tonight!' she sang brightly, 'To celebrate the last day of me being thirteen! We could get a takeaway!'

As if.

Unknown to her, dinner had already been arranged. Brian and I had slipped out earlier that day to buy fish. I wish I could tell you we strolled to the harbour and bartered with a white-bearded fisherman wearing a pair of yellow dungarees, but we didn't. We drove to Voli, Montenegro's version of Sainsbury's, and found our meal in the reduced aisle. Two large fish marked down heavily in price, probably due to their eyes being sealed shut and their abnormally swollen bellies.

I shared our dinner plans with Tessa, who was busy examining the scratches on her phone screen. I took the two dead fish from the bag and dangled them playfully by the tail in front of her face. I know. I can't help it. Sometimes, childish youthfulness just oozes out of me.

'Eeew. Gross!' she screeched, screwing up her face and backing away in disgust. 'Please say we're not having *that* for dinner. I hate fish; you know I do. Remember that time I got food poisoning at Riley Roger's fish "n" chips party?'

How ungrateful.

I was tempted to remind her that tomorrow wasn't all about her. That there was someone else present at her birth. 'What about me?' I wanted to say, 'This time, fourteen years ago, I was straddling an amniotic fluid-drenched beanbag. Panting like an overworked mule, having just spent twenty-eight hours pushing you out of my fanny. How about you give a thought to *that* miss I-hate-fish mardy pants?'

But I held my tongue.

I'd read somewhere that asking a child to picture their mother in labour causes undue distress and long-term brain damage, so instead I said, 'I bought you some of that nice mayonnaise you like. I'll mix it with garlic so you won't taste the fish'.

Later that evening, the three of us stood by the BBQ and dutifully watched as Brian prepared dinner. Gutting the fish and boring everyone senseless with his stories of when he worked in a Greek taverna for one summer fifty-eight years ago.

'Why are you leaving the head and tail on, Daddy?' Tessa asked, trying to sound interested but covering her mouth to conceal her urge to vomit.

'Because THAT'S Where all the flavour is!' beamed Brian-the-plumber-come-Michelin-star-chef.

He stuffed the fish bodies with fragrant herbs and tangy lemon, and trimmed the fins into the shape of a crocus. Then, to end his flamboyant performance, he rubbed flakes of pink sea salt between his fingers and thumb and sprinkled it elaborately over the skin. When the fish arrived at the teak picnic table fifteen minutes later, it was perfectly chargrilled, crispy and hot. It looked delicious.

It tasted foul.

'It smells a bit strong', said Sonny, sniffing the flesh and screwing up his nose. 'I'm starving. This isn't going to be enough for me'. He was right. By the time we'd picked out anything edible, we were left with no more than a teaspoon of fish flesh.

The rest of the meal was bones, pith, and thyme twigs.

The birthday

It is hard to find a decent birthday card in a foreign country. If you have kids, you will know what I mean when I say the card is everything. The card has to be right. Especially at fourteen.

Back home in New Zealand, I would have bought my daughter a card from the bookshop next to the library, but we were in Montenegro, so she got the next best thing.

On the morning of her birth, my now very grown-up fourteen-year-old opened a card featuring a giant blue-haired honey monster chewing a glittery doughnut. Inside, the words: 'Donut, you know it's your birthday?' Her reaction was one of trained politeness and confusion. She stared at the card for what seemed like ages before smiling weakly and saying, 'Thank you, everyone. That's really … nice. I love Rice Krispies'.

After the birthday breakfast, I suggested we visit Jaz Beach, the nearby famous seaside destination in Prijevor.

It is important to note that there are two parts to Jaz Beach, and both are very different. One end has fancy restaurants, modern music and tanned tourists who swim out to the enormous anchored inflatables; the other has a couple of fast-food shacks owned by miserable-looking locals who congregate outside to smoke cigarettes and swallow snot.

'Can't we go to the other side?' said Tessa, craning her neck as the car sped past the exit displaying the blinking neon Jaz Beach sign. 'It looks much more fun'.

Brian put his foot down. I rested my elbow out the open car window. 'No, thank you', I quipped. 'We didn't come all the way to

Montenegro to be part of some 18-30s naked psychedelic orgy'. I caught Sonny's reflection in the wing mirror.

He was panting.

The shittier, non-touristy part of Jaz Beach is easy enough to find. Turn off the main highway and follow the long unsealed road until you come to the end. You'll find a shack at the entrance to the beach which sells pizzas, ice creams, and beers.

The beach is pretty, but there is nothing to see. A bunch of horsehair parasols and white plastic sunbeds arranged neatly in rows line the shore, and for the price of a half-decent bottle of wine, you can rent one by the hour.

'Ohh! Can *we* get a bed and a parasol?' asked Tessa, using her birthday as a bribe.

'That might not be a bad idea, Liz', chimed Brian rubbing his hands up and down his chest like an ape with fleas. 'There's no shade, and the last thing I want is for my prickly heat to flare up'.

I stepped onto the sand, feigning deafness. I say sand; it wasn't sand at all. It was shingle. Tiny sharp pebbles, greyish-white in colour. Cruel, hard shingles that pierced the soft flesh of your feet. What a rip-off. *Where was the sand that every dreamy Montenegrin picture on Instagram boasted? Not here, that's for sure.*

Because I am intellectual and know all there is to know about politics and the likes, I told myself that the Montenegrin tourist board must have taken possession of all beach photos and doctored them using the vivid filter. Probably following orders from the Russian military.

Note to oneself. I must remember to use this example of scamminess in our next homeschooling lesson. It's essential that the children know how communist countries work.

I shifted my weight from one foot to the other and scanned the half-full beach, searching for a good spot to set up camp.

'There must be ... somewhere ... Ha! There! Bingo!'

I pointed to one of the beds at the end of a row, occupied by a randy young couple whose arms and legs were entwined and were snogging so hard their eyelids had turned purple. With no bed to the right of them, the shade from their parasol spilled over onto the shingle. Meaning that if we sat on the patch of sand right up close to their bed, we would be protected from the sun. For free! *Splendid!*

Sonny looked mortified.

'Oh, my God. Tell me you're not for real'. His cheeks were puce. 'There must be somewhere else. Can't we just sit in the car?'

Tessa looked puzzled. Brian took a sudden interest in a drone flying ten miles out to sea, and I scuttled across the beach to claim our spot. Going at full speed like one of those horn-eyed ghost crabs that only come out at night and run really fast.

I'm not sure about Montenegrin people. Maybe I'm wrong, and they're really quite lovely, but to me, they seem constantly pissed off. The men who work in petrol stations are gigantic, with faces that are weathered and stern, and the women who work in the supermarkets give you evil stares when you poke the reduced fish.

Suddenly aware that a family of four was moving next to their love nest, the couple on the bed untangled themselves and beheld us in disbelief. Horrified that we were so close to them. Using their excess paid-for parasol shade as if it were our own.

I ignored their rude glares and flicked my travel towel out in front of me. I was happy with our beach set-up. Because of me, my family would avoid getting skin cancer. And that's always a good thing. No one wants to go to the hospital with suspected melanoma. Especially not on a birthday.

Brian dug a hole in the stones with his fingers and made an indent for his bottom to fit into. He sat down. 'Wow! That's so clever, Daddy'. Tessa was genuinely impressed. 'Where did you learn to do that?'

I watched as he straightened his neck and grew two inches. Poor Brian. It must be exhausting being perfect. 'Basic survival training skills, Tess. Basic survival skills'.

Sonny was restless. He moaned that the sharp stones dug into his skin and irritated the acne on his back. *Sweet prince.* I suggested that he stop whining and go and make friends with the group of toddlers in front of us who were playing with an enormous blow-up unicorn. The acne was never mentioned again.

I won't lie; beaches aren't my favourite places. I live in dread of being asked to play games with my children.

I'm rubbish at games. There's only one game I like, and it's the one I used to play with Tessa when she was little. It was called Baby Bedtime.

'You be the baby, and I'll be the mummy', Tessa would say in a voice I didn't recognise. 'And we have to pretend it's nighttime. Okay, baby. Bedtime!' Then she'd put me to bed and tell me not to wake up, which I never did. Which made her frustrated and scared the beejeezus out of her.

More often than not, the game would end with her crying hysterically; pounding my chest with her chubby little fists. Peeling back my eyelids with her fingers. Screaming into my stone-like face, 'Noooo, baby! Wake up!! DON'T DIE, BABY!!'

After that, my daughter amended the rules.

The baby had insomnia, and the mummy slobbed in front of the telly and ate sweets. The name of the game was also changed; she called it Baby Smack Time.

I needn't have worried. Tessa, who had recently watched *Splash* and was now obsessed with Daryl Hannah, the fish woman, had her birthday entertainment schedule planned. She frolicked about in the sea and requested that Sonny take photos of her with her hair trailing out to the side as she floated in the water.

'Do I look like a mermaid?' she shouted back to shore.

The photo shoot ended abruptly when Sonny refused to take his role of David Bailey seriously and told his sister that she looked like one of the dead corpses in *The Poseidon Adventure*.

The afternoon wore on, and with everyone showing signs of irritation and dehydration, I decided to cheer things up. Surprise my birthday girl. Give her a special treat. I sat up on my towel and cleared my throat.

'Who wants to go and buy ice creams from the café?'

Brian's head did a 360-degree turn. Like Regan from *The Exorcist*. Tessa leapt to her feet.

'Me! I will, Mummy! Really? Come on, Sonny, we'll both go! Can I hold the money? Oh, thank you, Mummy, thank you!'

I snuck a look at the couple next to us, but their focus was elsewhere. They were sitting upright on their bed facing each other—engaged in a deep conversation. Probably discussing the cost of a vasectomy.

I had two twenty euro notes in my purse. I took one out and handed it over. 'Keep tight hold of this money until you get to the shop', I told Tessa, using my *Watch with Mother* voice because it was her birthday, and I wanted to show her that I wasn't always mean, 'And don't forget my change'.

Sonny was already halfway up the beach. Tessa remained where she was. She looked at the open purse and coyly walked her fingers up my arm. I flinched.

'What?'

'Can I get a Magnum?' She was using her baby voice. My jaw tightened.

It's her birthday, Liz. Smile, you miserable cow. 'Go on then … but only if there are no ice pops'.

Her eyes twinkled. She turned to go. Then stopped. *Jesus Christ, now what?*

'What if it's more?'

'It won't be more'.

'But what if it is?'

'It WON'T be'.

'But what if it is?'

My head felt like a punctured aerosol can. I reached into my purse and thrust the second note into her hand. 'Here!' I snapped impatiently. 'Now go. Before I change my mind'.

The woman on the bed next to us rolled to face us. She propped herself up on one elbow and raised one eyebrow. My daughter skipped happily away.

'And don't forget my change!' I called after her.

Within ten minutes, they were back. Having already devoured half of her white-coated Magnum, Tessa knelt on my towel and handed out the goodies.

'It was a bargain!' she gushed, 'They were only four euro fifty each!'

I heaved myself up from my towel, picking at the stones embedded into my fleshy calves.

'Where's my change?' I asked. I held out my hand and waited. Brian frowned and slid the wrapper from his ice cream.

It was windy. The parasols were blowing sideways.

Tessa reached into the pockets of her denim shorts and retrieved a two-euro coin. She handed it to me and then thrust her hand deeper. She stopped. I could see her fingers wiggling around in the denim. She frowned and pulled out an empty hand.

The couple next to us exchanged nervous glances.

'Hold this', she said, shoving her dripping ice cream into her brother's free hand. Panic spread over her face as she searched the other pocket. Nothing. The colour drained from her cheeks. 'I can't find it'.

Okay. We just need to pause the story for a minute... Have you ever recalled something so shameful that it makes your skin prickle with sweat? Well, this is me now. If I weren't writing this book, I would have buried this event deep into an old memory vault and denied it vehemently when my kids brought it up in the speeches at my funeral. But. I promised to tell you the truth. And as much as it

pains me to admit what I'm about to admit, it's important that we keep things
real. And honest. So here goes.

Sonny started mumbling and panicking, digging around in the sand like a Labrador, delving into the bags and checking under towels. 'You had it, Tess. I saw you. You had it!'

My blood began to boil. *Where. Was. My. Effing. Money?*

I heaved myself up from my towel and slid my feet into the only pair of shoes I owned—the flimsy brown sandals I'd bought in Thailand for a dollar. The ones with grimy insoles that made a sucking sound whenever I raised my arch.

'Let's see about this, shall we?' I grunted like a pig at an empty trough. I wrapped my sarong around my waist, ready to retrace the journey of the lost note. 'Let's. Just. See. About. THIS'.

Sonny gulped. The blood drained from Tessa's face. Brian got up from his towel, smiling apologetically at the couple next to us who had now unashamedly swung their legs over the edge of their bed and were facing us. All ears.

'Calm down, Liz', he soothed. 'It's only …' I spun to confront him. Two blasts of steam shot from my snout. His words evaporated. He lowered himself back down. '…I'll wait here with Sonny and look after the stuff'.

Off I went.

Barging up the shingly beach. Forcing crowds of oncoming locals to part company and make way for me. Like Moses when he reached the Red Sea.

'I'm sorry, Mummy', said Tessa. 'Please don't worry. I'm sure we'll find it'. Her voice wobbled as she panted to keep pace.

'Yes, you will, missy', I sputtered like a petrol-starved engine. 'And let me tell you, if you *don't* find that money, I will march you back to the café, and you can tell the lady that she short-changed you'.

Blimey. What a thought. Facing a Montenegrin honey monster and accusing her of fraud.

The search along the gravel path began.

Tessa half-heartedly kicked at the dust. Keeping one eye on the road and the other on her unpredictable mother, bent over crooked, shuffling along like a homeless crone. Picking up dirty random stones and then disappointedly shaking her head in a hideous exaggerated fashion and throwing them back to the ground.

At one point, Sonny made an appearance and offered to replace the lost twenty euros with the Minecraft money he'd made with his fake Facebook account. I refused. 'This is a matter of carelessness', I chided. 'And a lesson needs to be learned'.

What an old bag.

No blade of grass was left unruffled. No stone unturned. We made Sherlock Holmes look like an amateur. It was hot; we were thirsty, and I used whatever spit I had in my mouth to bark orders at my careless daughter. (The one whose birthday it was.) An hour or so later, feeling nauseous from the heat and unable to muster the courage to face the woman in the ice cream shop, I grudgingly called off the search.

'Forget it', I sulked, picking up one last crisp packet and looking inside. 'It's gone. Let's go back to the beach. We'll have bread and water for our tea tonight.' I turned to leave.

'I promise to pay you back, Mummy'. Tessa's voice was small and quiet. 'I'll use Uncle Dave's money'.

Sometimes I wish I could slap myself in the face with a reduced fish. I knew that I was in the wrong that day. I knew I was acting like a spoiled brat who needed to act her age and not her shoe size, but I still carried on. And because I'd gone so far and was trying to make a point of being angry, I chose to ignore my daughter's apology and instead made my way back along the stone dirt road with speed.

And that's when it happened.

Looking back, I think it was the birthday gods paying me back. Teaching me a lesson for being so penny-pinching and tight.

'Arrrgggg!!' Crash. Skid. Bang. Wallop.

The front of my wafer-thin sandal gave way. Doubled in on itself, leaving my feet uncovered and vulnerable.

With nothing to hold my toes in place, my foot flew forward and plunged into a cavernous pothole in the middle of the road. I lost my balance and wobbled, crashed, head first, into a makeshift grave of Montenegrin rocks, breaking two of my toes and tearing the flesh on my arms and legs to shreds.

The pain surged through me. The world spun. Tessa stood over me. Her mouth wide open. Unsure what to do next. My legs were bleeding. My feet looked deformed.

All this for twenty sodding euros.

'Heeelp me', I wailed, my face hideously contorted. (Best to cause as much panic as possible in situations like this, I always think.) I lay there. Curled up in a ball. Wallowing in self-pity. Imagining how I might die—melting into the Montenegrin dirt like the Wicked Witch of the West. Or worse still, swallowed by a giant honey monster with doughnut breath.

Tessa sprang to action, suddenly seeming much older than her fourteen years.

'Wait here', she said. 'And don't move. I'll go and get Daddy!' Then she ran away as fast as possible towards the beach, never looking back. Leaving me alone in the ditch. With my mangled feet.

I closed my eyes and squeezed out a few tears. Filled with guilt and regret and broken toes. Watching as my daughter's blonde ponytail disappeared around the corner. My heart throbbed.

My hero. My rescuer. My baby bedtime girl.

The words she happily sang the night before rang in my ears.

'This will be one birthday that I'll NEVER forget!'

No, my darling. I doubt very much you ever will.

CHAPTER TWELVE
CROATIA

My son was born at home on 21 June in Bath, England. Midsummer's night. The shortest night of the year.

If you are a witch and a cool hippie like me who believes that the moon is a woman with a giant bald head and grants you wishes when you give birth to a son on the night of the summer solstice, you will appreciate what I am about to share.

That night, while straddling the soggy denim beanbag in the front bedroom of our 1950s corner detached house, still off my face on gas and air, I swore from that day forward, we would celebrate the arrival of our son by doing something mythical and magical.

And weird.

'Each year …' I slurred sentimentally into Brian's contorted face, clutching handfuls of his hair so he couldn't pull away, 'we will give thanks. Do something brilliant for our little boy … on the night of his birth …. Like what Jenny Cummings from Glastonbury does …. She floats candles down a stream every new moon and makes a wish … swears by it she does …. One time, she wished she had more money … and the next day, a rebate turned up from the council …. Yes … that's what we'll do ….'

The midwife was kind and reassuring. She brought Brian a cup of tea and told him not to worry. Said that my incoherent babbling was a common side effect of the drugs and to ignore everything I was saying because I was talking utter shite.

But she was wrong. I never forgot that midsummer's night promise.

If Jenny Cummings could float candles down a river and make wishes to the moon, so would I. *And* I might even let my children drink watered-down red wine, too.

A year later, on a wet and miserable English June evening, we took our one-year-old son, wrapped in baby-Jesus swaddling clothes and crept out of the house, making sure not to set the automatic light sensor off on the garage as we did so. The woman next door took her neighbourhood watch duties very seriously. The last thing we needed was to stop and explain to Betty from number eight where we were going at such a late hour.

Carrying only a few bare essentials: three pieces of bolster wood, a pen knife, some candles and a couple of packets of barbeque beef-flavoured Hula Hoops from the co-op, we climbed into the car and set off on our very first pilgrimage. Us three. In search of ancient candle floating water. In our RAV4.

We parked at the back of Sainsbury's Express. Next to the aqueduct.

'This is the spot!' announced Brian, turning the key and banging the top of the steering wheel triumphantly as if he'd just discovered the cure for cancer. 'This'll do nicely!'

I beamed.

Brian knew all the good places. Back then, when we were still young and fresh, I thought everything my husband said was right and funny.

Stepping over the alcoholic dossers that slept on the floor between the cash point machine and the trolly park, we silently made our way down to the local canal. I would like to tell you that we strolled in the twilight with nothing but our love to keep us warm, but I can't.

It was pissing down and miserable.

Twice I nearly tripped and dropped our wriggling son into the water while looking for a suitable place to build and launch our candle carriers.

Eventually, we found it. An out-of-the-way spot where we wouldn't be disturbed. Standing under an old oak tree by the edge of the water, sheltering from the rain and dressed in nothing but linen robes and my Berlei breastfeeding bra, I watched dotingly as my very handy-and-extremely-manly husband whittled away with his penknife to make three little boats.

I can't remember where we got the wood from; I think we nicked it from Betty's shed.

'There', said Brian proudly, holding the finished result out in front of his nose as if he was Geppetto and had just carved a real-life boy out of wood. 'Let's just add the finishing touch ....' I waited patiently. Observed with interest as he melted candle wax onto the wood so that the Ikea tea light would stay in place.

Genius.

'Look, Sonny!' I cooed. 'Look what your daddy's made for us! Three little wishing boats out of wood .... Isn't he clever? I bet your friend Freddy from Moovin' and Groovin' hasn't got a daddy as good yours!'*Actually, Freddy's real daddy remains a mystery. Even to his mum.*

Brian's smile spread to both ears. We lit our candles and pushed the vessels out into the water. Whispering our wishes as they floated away.

The birthday boat ritual continued for seven years. Right up until we moved to New Zealand.

For those of you who don't know, New Zealand is in the Southern hemisphere. Meaning that our boy's birthday was now on the shortest night of the year. Midwinter's night. The winter solstice. Symbolising death and darkness and ugly spiders.

No longer holding the same appeal, we decided to end the birthday ritual. Call it a day. I can't say I was that bothered—in a way, I was relieved. As the kids got older, the yearly event got harder. Friends were introduced, picnics requested. And anyway, I had fallen out with Jenny Cummings four years ago when she left her husband to run a pub in Spain with the rep from the crystal shop.

The tradition ended. The birthday boat ritual faded into a distant memory.

And Jenny Cummings was never mentioned again.

Ten years later …

Croatia is divine.

The sea is turquoise, the roofs are deep orange, and the coastline is rugged and beautiful. Everything is exactly what it says on the packet.

Imagine my delight when I realised our time in Croatia coincided with my son's seventeenth birthday. That we could once again celebrate his joyous arrival in the Northern Hemisphere. At last, I could bring the tradition back to life. Resurrect the dead. Call forth the summer solstice moon with the massive head and love for candles.

*As a side note, you may have noticed that both my children share the same birth month. It's true. My husband and I only ever have sex in September. We believe in baby batching. Getting it all done and dusted and out of the way by Christmas. I highly recommend it.

Because I am a snob who thinks it's tacky to stay where other tourists stay, I made sure our Croatian accommodation was in the middle of the countryside. Miles from nowhere. Nice and cheap.

'Split looks like a fun city to celebrate a birthday', said Sonny wistfully as our Fiat Uno rental car sped through the vibrant coastal city. He pressed his forehead against the window and eyeballed a gang of bare-chested youths walking along the street with their arms draped across each other's shoulders. Young lads enjoying a dirty weekend with their mates. Swigging beer from green Heineken cans and smoking fags.

I pulled down the sun visor and spoke through the mottled rectangle mirror.

'Just wait and see what I have planned for you!' I said, widening my eyes and nodding. 'There's not a boy in the kingdom who'll be able to say he celebrated his seventeenth birthday the way you're about to. Not one'.

Sonny heaved a heavy sigh and closed his eyes. Tessa bit her lip. And Brian turned on the radio.

We were staying in the small village of Hrvace, about twenty-odd miles from Split.

Hrvace is lovely. The fields are full of poppies and cowslips, and there's a church with a bell and little shops where friendly locals stand outside and smile. It's beautiful. Quaint. Quiet and unspoiled. Like stepping back in time. Brian and I loved it. The kids said it resembled a morgue.

We were walking along the lanes admiring the hedgerows because there was nothing else to do.

'It reminds me of *Worzel Gummidge*!' I said gaily, hoping that someone would ask me to elaborate on my childhood memories so I could bore them for hours with my favourite television programmes and then tell them all about how we only ever ate beans on toast in our house because we were poor and would never have been able to afford to go on an amazingly wonderful and very generous trip such as this.

Nobody said a word.

For those who don't know, *Worzel Gummidge* is a British TV series about two children, John and Jane, who go on holiday with their father. Don't ask me where the mother was, I have no idea. I think she ran away with a bloke who kept birds down his pants.

The family stay in a caravan on a farm in the middle of the English countryside: Scatterbrook Farm. It was always sunny and warm at

Scatterbrook. Even in the *Worzel Gummidge* Christmas Special, the trees were in full bloom.

One day, John and Jane go out exploring (because it was the 1970s and kids didn't have anxiety disorders about going outside back then), and much to their delight, they discover a talking scarecrow. Worzel. The children and Worzel go on many adventures together, frolicking through the yellow barley and getting up to mischief at the local summer fare.

Terrifyingly, Worzel also could decapitate himself. But that's a whole different story and one we won't explore today.

Hrvace, in Croatia, was like living in that TV series. Like staying at Scatterbrook Farm. Never has anywhere else in the world evoked such memories of childhood. Hrvace felt safe and calm and peaceful. The innocence. The crows. The old tractors. The people who have time to stop and chat. The men with carrots as noses.

You could stick touristy, Split up your arse. Give me Hrvace any day.

If I were to show you a picture of the Airbnb we were staying in and then tell you the cost, you'd probably have a heart attack. Which wouldn't be ideal, so I won't. The place was an absolute bargain. It was a newly renovated farmhouse with whitewashed walls and distressed floorboards. Tall skinny windows with shutters painted a soft blue colour, like a blackbird's egg, looked out onto a large secluded garden with an almond tree at one end and a wild cherry tree at the other. It was magical—the kind of place you see on the front of The Lady magazine.

We were so happy. Everything was perfect. There was a fully equipped kitchen for me, a squishy comfy bed for Bri and a fifty-inch flat-screen TV wired up to the internet for the kids.

Things couldn't be better.

With my son's seventeenth birthday looming, I made it a priority to find a place to launch the celebration boats. Luckily I didn't have to wait too long.

One morning, as I was leaning on my elbows out of the kitchen window and singing to the birds like Snow White, I spotted an old barn standing in the middle of a wild meadow (probably where the Worzels of the village took their Aunt Sallys for a bit of hanky panky).

To the right of the barn was a stream. It wasn't a particularly wide stream, but it was long and meandered around the back of a few houses, stretching the entire length of the village. Next to the stream was a narrow well-trodden path.

I had found it!

The sacred water. The place where the wish-granting flame would burn brightly. The creek where I would perform the sacrificial yeartide ritual and give thanks for having been blessed with a prodigy son who had gained his purple belt in Karate by the time he was twelve and could play "Swan Lake" on the piano without even looking.

The day of the birthday

I hate my kids at times. Especially my son. He's so bloody ungrateful.

'Happy Birthday to you! Happy birthday to you! Happy birthday, dear …' We'd burst into his bedroom in full song, Tessa, Brian, and me, showering him with balloons and throwing bits of screwed-up toilet tissue into his face. (I usually buy confetti, but I wouldn't know where to get that in Croatia.)

'Happy Birthday, my love!!' I gushed, secretly hoping that someone would remember to ask about how hard my labour had been seventeen years earlier.

My son opened one eye and squeezed out a pathetic half-smile. He mumbled something about the time and his bladder and then disappeared into the bathroom with his phone.

Pff. What a waste of money. He obviously doesn't know the price of quilted three-ply toilet rolls in Croatia.

Sonny doesn't cope well with celebrations. Especially ones where the attention is all on him. He's one of those weird kids who say, 'I prefer other people's birthdays to my own'.

I used to think this was because he was a nice child who preferred giving over receiving, but he isn't. He's just a thankless brat who is never happy with what he gets.

One Christmas, when he was fifteen, we bought him a Buzz Lightyear mask and put it in his stocking. He wore it all morning while opening his presents. It was a miracle. Transformed the whole day. Even though you could see from the slump of his shoulders that he was massively disappointed with every gift bestowed upon him, all we saw was a big beaming Buzz mask flashing its sparkly white grin at us. Expressing gratitude and cheerfulness. It was marvellous.

Stupid of me, really .... I can't believe I didn't think to bring the mask along with us on this trip.

After we had done the obligatory waffles for breakfast, afternoon ice cream in the square, and pizza for dinner (we even splurged and bought a family-size one, and they're not cheap), I announced the evening plans.

'And now!' I said theatrically, standing in front of the TV and doing that thing with my hands that Liza Minelli does when she performs *Cabaret*. 'The ritual we've ALL been waiting for! Drum roll, please!! Drrrrrr … the ceremonial candle-floating experience where wishes ALWAYS come true! HURRAY!'

(I thought about adding a few can-can kicks but decided that might be going a bit far.)

Tessa blushed. Sonny reached for the remote control, looked at it and then put it back down again. His eyes avoided mine.

'Yeah … the thing is … I don't really want to do that. Not *this* year. Logan is doing a live interview at 11.00 p.m., and I don't really want to miss it'.

How rude. How bloody fucking rude.

I let out a long and heavy breath.

Tessa picked at the nail on her little toe.

'Unbe-lievable', I said, placing my thumb and index finger into the corners of my eyes and shaking my head like people do in films when they're annoyed but are trying to remain dignified. I inhaled deeply. 'I bet there isn't a young lad on this planet who wouldn't give his right arm to spend his birthday floating wood down a river in the moonlight with his family. What a shame that my son would rather look at a screen. Worshipping a sicko. How very. Dis. A. Point. Ing'.

'Actually, Mummy, Logan publicly apologised for doing that thing in the Japanese woods'.

'Shut up, you, and stop picking your toes, or you'll end up like a hobbled cripple'.

The spiel continued.

'This is who you *are*, Sonny', I said, stretching the words out to give them more meaning. 'This is your *birthright*. It's what we do. It's midsummer's night, the night you were born. We *always* do this'.

Luckily, no one mentioned that we hadn't done it for the past eight years.

Sonny rammed his hands into his pockets and scowled. 'Fine', he said miserably. 'We'll go'.

'OMG, Sonny', muttered Tessa. 'Whatever you do, don't Snapchat it'.

Under cover of darkness, carrying the little black rucksack packed with wood, candles and other ritual-performing essentials, we set off for the Croatian stream.

Once out of view of any law-abiding citizens who might take it upon themselves to call the police and report four pyromaniacs, Brian took out his Primark pen knife (the one he'd smuggled through countless airports by wrapping it in his underpants and stowing it inside his sleeping bag) and began to carve quickly and intently. His lips stretched tight across his teeth.

We gathered around him. We were in a field next to the stream. The grass was long and damp.

'Can I have a go?' asked Sonny. His interest suddenly sparked by the sight of a lethal weapon. He pulled his hood down and eyed the knife greedily. 'I'm brilliant at carving'.

Brian puffed out his cheeks like an inflated toad and held the blade at arm's length.

'Absolutely not. Knives are very dangerous weapons and should be treated with respect. Only proper men can use knives like this'.

Pompous old bastard.

I was about to argue that, at seventeen, our son was more than capable of yielding an imitation Swiss Army knife, but then I remembered that kid on Facebook who had aichmomania and massacred his entire family. 'Stand back, my angel', I warned, blocking his path with my arm. 'Daddy will cut the wood. You can just watch'.

Brian filled his lungs and clenched his fist, causing the veins in his arm to protrude. 'I didn't get an "O" Level in woodwork for nothing', he bragged, digging the blade further into the grain with such force that it almost went right through and punctured his left palm.

Men are so annoying. Honestly. They drive me insane. Why can't they just get on and do something without expecting a standing ovation?

Can you imagine if every time a woman performed a task, she stood there with her hands bouncing upwards and her eyebrows raised like Bruce Forsyth, waiting for the room to explode into rapturous applause? 'Hey? Hey? Made dinner for four people, emptied the washing machine, cleaned the fridge and wiped the slobber from the dog's chops. Didn't she do well?'

After many oohs and aahs and you're-really-good-at-making-little-wooden-boats-and-you-should-have-been-a-carpenter compliments, the vessels were almost complete.

'Good job, Daddy', said Tessa, who had spent the last ten minutes shining the torch under her chin, making an annoying popping sound with her cheeks and hadn't even been watching.

'Just … one … more thing ….' Brian reached into the bag and pulled out a roll of aluminium foil. Holding it between both knees, he expertly ripped off a few small pieces with which he lined each boat, making sure to smooth out any shiny silver creases with his thumb. 'Ta-da!' He handed me my boat.

I looked at it and blinked.

If I was the kind of woman who wanted to belittle her husband in front of his children and punish him for having kept us waiting in a field full of cow shit for an hour in the dark, I might have said: 'What the hell is *this*? Call that a boat? That's rubbish! A baby could do better than that. That's not a boat. It looks more like a wooden heroin bong to me'.

But I'm not, and I don't, so I didn't.

Besides, no child likes to hear their mother talking casually about opioid narcotics. Not on the day of their birth.

'That's amazing!' I cried. 'I love it! It reminds me of a miniature Cutty Sark'.

This birthday tradition was never meant to be competitive or fierce. It was supposed to be a gentle coming-together-of-souls. A bonding experience. So, where did it all go wrong?

I looked at my family standing at the water's edge, each clutching their wooden water wagon. Snarling. Drooling. Panting like a pack of bull terriers on the lead. Biting at the muzzle. Ready to throw their wish-maker into the water with no other goal than to win.

'Let the games commence!' I whooped jubilantly, trying to lighten the mood and be like Keith Chegwin when he hosted *It's a Knockout* in Scarborough.

We lit our candles. The ritual began. Plop. Push. Whoosh. They were off! We trotted alongside our buoyant boats excitedly. Carefully avoiding rabbit holes and stinging nettles, urging our candle not to die.

What a sodding disaster.

Two minutes into it, all but one of the boats sank. Pulled to the bottom of the riverbed like the *Titanic* but without the chandelier and the fiddlers. While my husband's flame-on-wood charged ahead, all that remained of my children's and mine were three pieces of blackened tinfoil. Floating downstream, sadly.

Brian didn't care.

He ran excitedly alongside his winning wood, cheering it on as it whizzed downstream at a rate of knots, the candle still blazing like the Olympian torch. I shone my torch at his head. Hoping to dazzle him in the eyes and cause him to trip over and fall into the river and drown. *Show off.* I bet he'd used one of those candles that never go out. The ones that rich kids have at bouncy-world birthday parties.

How very shit and wanky crap.

Tessa stared into the murky water and shook her head in disbelief as the lining from her boat wrapped itself around a clump of vegetation. 'If fish eat tin foil, it kills them ....' her wobbly words trailed off.

'Well, that was epic'. Sonny swung his Goliath-sized foot into a sod of grass with such force that the muddy turf flew up into the sky and landed with a thump behind us. 'What a waste of time! I *hate* it here .... This has got to be the worst birthday *ever!*' He slammed his fist into the opposite palm and scowled.

Un. Believable.

If I was the kind of mother who wasn't very nice and wanted to make her son's birthday even worse than it already was, I might have said something like: 'Shut your face, you whinging little tosser. I opened my cervix for you. Pushed you out with nothing but a bit of nitrous oxide to ease the pain. And for what? All so you can dishonour Queen Mab and the crystals with your evil ways? I don't think so, son.'

But I'm not, and it wasn't possible, so I didn't.

Besides, no child wants to imagine their mother with her legs spread.

Not on his seventeenth birthday.

I gave it one last attempt. 'Come on!' I shrieked, all hyper like Winifred Banks after too many sherries. 'The night's not over yet! Let's all run after Daddy's boat! Yes! Let's do that! It can still be fun!'

Nobody moved. Tessa's eyes went to Sonny. He took out his phone and checked the time.

Who was I trying to kid? Fun? Fun? You call running after a middle-aged man in glasses who won't even let you have a go with his penknife fun?

I didn't want to chase him and his piece of wood any more than they did. Fun to me was reading about what Rose West did in the cellar with Fred.

I was done. Defeated. Tired. I turned to walk away. Regretting ever starting this stupid tradition.

'I don't like it when she says fun, do you?' Tessa whispered to Sonny. 'It reminds me of Sue Banger, from the homeschool spelling Bee'.

Brian never came home that night.

The last we saw of him, he was jogging along the riverbank on the other side of the village, heading for the shores of the Adriatic Sea. Chasing his boat with the inextinguishable candle.

'Look at my beauty go!' he cried faintly before turning a corner and disappearing out of view. 'That's what happens when you balance weight with ratiooooo. It's about the physics, Sonny—centrifugal force … It's what makes me a winnnnerrrrr ….'

Croatia is gorgeous.

You must go. And when you do, make sure you visit Hrvace.

Take a walk by the stream in the meadow. Look deep into the water. You'll find a piece of old rotten wood. Pick it up and wish on it. My treat. And remember. If you, your daughter, or any woman you know falls pregnant and is told that the baby is due on 21 June?

Put a fucking cork in your fanny. Cross your legs. Hold it in. Do whatever it takes, but do NOT give birth to that child.

Not for at least another week.

CHAPTER THIRTEEN
POMPEII

During our first stint in Italy, we didn't manage to go far south. After we'd visited Venice and Rome, marvelled at the toppling tower in Pisa and taken the kids to Verona to show them where their father proposed to me, it was time to leave. With so many places still on our list, we decided to return to Italy and cross off a few more must-dos.

For me, one of those must-dos was somewhere I'd longed to see for years. *Pompeii*. The mysterious city that the world knew so little about.

Ever since Primary school, I'd been intrigued by Pompeii. The bodies, the dead dog, the ash. The city that had been frozen in time in 79 AD. And now here we were. About to see it for ourselves. And I couldn't wait.

We were staying in the charming town of Formicola in the Province of Caserta, which is within striking distance of Naples and Pompeii, making it the perfect base for exploring the Southern tip of Italy.

Formicola is pretty.

The town has a small market square flanked by pale pink and yellow-painted townhouses. There are a few simple shops and a café that offers terrace tables, perfect for those parents who sneak out in the early morning and leave their teenagers sweating and hungry in bed while they indulge in a shared pastry and a couple of shots of strong Italian coffee.

I'm not fond of the term 'bucket list'. It reminds me of mini cruises and men in long white socks. But certain destinations *need* to be on a bucket list. And Pompeii is one of them. No human being should kick the bucket without seeing Pompeii. Nor should they be embarrassed about wearing socks with sandals. It's the only way to avoid blisters.

I was determined to dress appropriately for my visit to Pompeii.

When the day came, I wore my ankle-length black dress (the one that hadn't been washed since India) and my brown and gold headband (the one that makes me look like Liz Taylor in *Cleopatra*). All I needed now was a toga-clad Richard Burton to invite me to ride upon his steely chariot.

'It's nine o'clock. If we don't leave now, we're going to hit traffic'.

Grumpy pants Brian. His untamed eyebrows knitted together in a huff. Waiting in the car with the engine running. Hunched over the steering wheel, squinting at the satnav. Muttering about second and third exits and cheap fuel opportunities.

In case no one has ever told you, it's worth driving to Naples—if only to experience the colourful entertainment along the roadside. Don't bother taking a book for the journey. You won't need it. There is plenty to see along the way.

Almost every layby on the road leading to Naples is occupied by a woman of the night. Or, in this case, a woman of ten past nine in the morning. Young and old, tight and baggy, beautiful and squeezed. All selling their wares. Laying seductively across the bonnets of cars. Facing the oncoming traffic with their bloomers blowing in the wind, hoping to score a quickie from a bloke in a Fiat Panda on his way to work.

Harlots. Strumpets. Working girls. Prozzies.

I'm all for supporting women. I love them, but I'm sorry, proper or not, I'm yet to meet a woman on Earth who doesn't find the profession of selling sex for money fascinating, me included. Especially me.

Very much me.

I turned and pressed my face to the window like one of those big fat rubber-lipped catfish that suck algae from fish tanks. My eyes widened. No way was I missing this.

'Why are we driving so slow?' questioned Tessa, suddenly aware that the satnav had been muted and both her parents and brother were gawking out the window like a bunch of pervs. She craned her neck. 'What are they doing? Is it a car boot sale? Shall we stop and give them some money?'

Sonny sniggered. The penny dropped. Tessa shrunk back into her seat, her cheeks flushed.

'Oh, my God, can you all just stop staring? It's so embarrassing. That is SO disrespectful to females and human rights. Put *Harry Potter* on, Daddy. We're up to chapter seven. Daddy? Hello? Daddy?'

She was right, of course. It was wrong to stare. These women aren't to be ogled at. But I couldn't help it. Nine months of sharing a room with two teenagers had left me high and dry. Gagging. Desperate. Not since *Band of Gold* aired on the BBC in the 1990s had I witnessed so much nooky.

For the last thirty minutes of the journey, the car crawled along the highway at a snail's pace.

I was engrossed.

My children were damaged.

And miraculously, Brian's short-range vision loss corrected itself instantly.

The modern-day town of Pompeii is not dissimilar to that of Blackpool in the North of England. Only without the candy floss and the corkscrew. There are a bunch of tacky-looking restaurants, market stalls selling far too much plastic, and a couple of dodgy-looking hotels that look as though they are run by the Mafia.

My first impression wasn't good.

Shit. Maybe I've overdressed. I knew I should have worn my green cargo pants—the ones that make me look like Demi Moore in G.I. Jane.

Tessa, on the other hand, couldn't have been happier.

'Ohhh, Sonny! This isn't going to be boring after all! There are shops and everything! Hurray! I can spend that $100 Uncle Dave sent me for Christmas!'

Selfish girl.

Unbeknownst to her, we had used that hundred-dollar birthday bill to pay for the visas in Vietnam. That was long gone. I pursed my lips into the shape of a cat's backside.

'Stop screeching', I snapped. 'We're here to pay our respects to the dead people of Italy. Not spend money on shoddy mass-produced tat'.

After cruising the strip looking for a cheap place to park, we finally found it on a dirty scrap of wasteland at the rear of Ristorante Vesuvio. The owner had made a makeshift sign and propped it against the wall next to the kitchen door. "All day parking Ten Euro", the sign said. I think it was painted in mob blood.

'Why can't we park where everyone else is parking …?' Tessa looked longingly back at the shops.

'Yeah', added Sonny desperately, 'Please don't park here; it's miles away from everything'.

The car tyres rumbled as we drove down onto the dry, gravelly parking lot, past the shifty-looking guy guarding the entrance. I mouthed 'Grazie' out of the closed window and gave him a friendly wave. He flashed a gold-toothed smile at Sonny and winked. *What a nice chap.*

Silly children. Hadn't they learned by now? Money is money. If leaving the car miles from nowhere means saving four Euros, then so be it.

'It won't take us long to walk to the old city', I said as if I knew anything about distance and time. 'And we could all do with a little bit of exercise'.

I heaved out of the car and wiped the sweat from my armpits with the back of my hand, grateful that I had chosen to wear my sleeveless dress. *How clever of me.* Everyone knows that on hot days like this, it is essential that the underarm skin remain dry and well-ventilated. Otherwise, you end up with those hideous chicken pimples that sting when you shave. I made a mental note to pass on this information to Tessa next time we have one of our girly question-and-answer sessions.

I stretched my gaze into the distance, up beyond the walls of ancient Pompeii. Feasting my eyes on the slender, elegant church spires that stood alongside swollen-bellied buildings, topped with powdery lime green domes.

My tummy jumped.

This was magnificent. Breathtakingly beautiful.

I'll be honest with you. I'm not a fan of popular places—tourist traps. If we do go to them (which is rare), I tend to expect the worst. That way, I'm never disappointed. Although Pompeii was somewhere I had always wanted to see, I secretly expected the ruins to be a bit crap. Like one of those model railway villages you find on the West Coast of Cornwall. The kind that advertises replicas of tin mines, but then when you get there, there's nothing but a few measly plastic dolls leaning against a house made of lollypop sticks.

But I was wrong. Very wrong.

Ancient Pompeii was no model village. No tourist gimmick. This was a beautiful half-fallen city that sat majestically under the watchful eye of Mount Vesuvius—flanked by scorched hills, upright cypress trees and ancient pines. A magnificent piece of preserved history with pathways, streets, and walls wrapped around ancient buildings.

Leaving the car securely locked (Brian checked it at least ten times), we walked along the strip towards the entrance of the ancient ruins.

I was in a world of my own. A beautiful world filled with Romans and togas and crowns made of thorns. And me, a damson in a dirty black dress trailing along the dusty cobblestones—gliding up the street on a set of well-oiled castors towards my gladiator in the pay booth.

Brian cleared his throat.

'I wasn't expecting it to be like this', he said irritably because he was thirsty from the drive, and I'd told him not to bother bringing any water because we could stop for a cup of tea on the way, but we hadn't. He scowled and cocked his head towards the rows of market stalls manned mainly by men. Italian men. Good-looking hunky Italian men. 'It's all about money at the end of the day, isn't it? How sad'.

Then he stopped and tutted and shook his head like old men do when they all get together and reminisce about the war.

Jesus Christ. Brian, the Socrates Scouser, hath spoken.

I was about to remind him that even in the olden days, Romans would have had market stalls to sell things like ancient rubber and batteries. How else did they build all those roads? But I was interrupted by Tessa's whining.

'It's not fair …. I wish I had Uncle Dave's money with me. There's a pair of Converse back there for eight dollars. Real ones. I love Converse. Millie Bobby Brown has twenty-eight pairs'.

I looked to Brian for support, but he had gone. Off on a mission. Pounding along the pavement with his neck jowls swinging like a turkey. Past the handsome stall-holders. His nylon New Zealand rugby shirt stretched tight across his belly.

'Hey! Hey, Kiwi! You from New Zealand, man? Greta cricket, huh?' A hawker with an armful of selfie sticks called out to him from across the street.

At this point, you must understand something. My husband has never watched a game of New Zealand cricket in his life. Not ever. He hates the game.

He thinks it's boring and slow. Nor was he born in New Zealand. Meaning he has no right to call himself a Kiwi.

Brian raised his eyebrows and added to the banter. 'Yeah, mate!' he shouted. 'We've had a good season, that's for sure!' Then he looked away and began fiddling with the straps on his daypack, mumbling something about wickets and runs and Pakistan.

Bloody liar. Sodding Liverpudlian fake liar with his little grey shorts. We've had a good season? What the hell?

'Why does Daddy never tell anyone that we were born in England?' asked Tessa, trotting behind and genuinely curious.

I wanted to tell her that it was because everyone hates the Brits, especially the Italians, who always lose to us at footy. But I thought this might give her anxiety issues and cause her to turn to drugs when she reached eighteen, so I sucked in my cheeks and answered with kindness.

'Shut up. No one likes children who ask impertinent questions. And stop stooping over like an earwig, or you'll end up wearing a back brace'.

It costs money to enter Pompeii.

I can't remember how much exactly, but if my memory serves me rightly, kids get a discount ,and oldies also get a bit of dosh knocked off. (As I said, don't hold me to this; my memory is shocking.)

You can also take a tour. If you want to. Pay money to a guide who will tell you all about the place.

'Let's do it', said Brian. 'It's not every day that we come to see Pompeii!'

He was striding purposefully towards the pretty olive-skinned woman sitting inside a glass ticket kiosk. Chocolate brown eyes and long black hair. Like an Italian Rapunzel. She smiled when she saw him and tilted her dainty nose upwards.

'Allo', she drawled. 'Good Morneen'.

No way, José. Not happening, matey.

Ramming my elbow into his ribs, I pushed in front of Brian and thrust a fifty euro note through the window's opening.

'Family of four, please', I said, showing my teeth to the Italian beauty. 'Me and my husband are seventy, both my children are under ten, and we don't need a tour, thank you. Not today. I've done my research. I know all there is to know about everything'.

The woman took my money. She seemed confused. She batted her lashes and opened her mouth; rested her moist little tongue on top of her plump bottom lip. Brian looked aroused. The kids were in the corner, crouched down. Pretending to read the toilet sign that was written in Italian.

I snatched my change and thanked Rapunzel.

'Come on, little children', I cried softly and frailly. 'Come and help Granny and Grandad up the ramp'. Then I helped myself to a handful of free maps and flounced out of the foyer. Closing the door behind me.

It's funny what your mind does to you, isn't it? Ancient Pompeii was nothing how I'd imagined it to be. It was far better.

I had envisaged a pile of bricks lined up in a row, numbered and behind a rope. Exhibit No 1: a piece of old stone. Exhibit No 6: the hem from a maiden's dress. But no, Pompeii was the real McCoy. Like being immersed in a romantic novel that you could see, smell, feel, and touch.

While the kids played zombie hide and seek in Exhibit No 12, Brian and I picked our way around the ruins. Marvelling at the perfectly placed pebble stones that lined the streets—taking lots of photos of the raised drinking bowls that had been left dry for centuries, admiring the stone that had been worn down and made smooth by those who had knelt to drink from it thousands of years earlier.

'Imagine what life would have been like in 79 AD. Before the volcano erupted and everyone was mummified', I called over my shoulder to Brian, hoping he would partake in my role-play and look at me the way he had looked at Rapunzel in the ticket booth.

He wasn't listening.

He had his head under a rock, examining a piece of metal that he claimed was a vital part of the city's sewerage infrastructure.

My thoughts went to the women who, thousands of years earlier, had traipsed along those cobbled roads, lugging their heavy bricks to market while their husbands, strong and handsome, stood by, watching—eating grapes and chatting to their pals about how liberating it was to wear a toga without a loincloth.

'When can we go and see the bodies?' The kids were getting hot and bored. *Damn it. Why do they always have to spoil everything?* I had planned on saving the corpses until the end of the day.

'I think I saw an ice cream stall at the top of the hill behind the arena', I lied, knowing full well that there was no such thing. 'Go and see if it's open, and then come back, and I'll give you some money'.

Brian said he'd go with them. They left.

At last. Time to myself.

The House of Menander is one of ancient Pompeii's wealthiest and most magnificent houses. It was owned by Quintus Poppaeus, who was said to have been related to Emperor Nero's second wife (that raving nutter who set fire to Rome).

Historians and archaeologists have painstakingly and preciously restored the building, and as such, the security around it is red hot. Ramped up to the max.

Standing at the entrance to Menander House was a female guard. Huge she was. At least ten feet tall. A Herculean heifer wearing crimplene trousers and a scowl that would melt metal.

Towering over the entrance like a giant ogre.

She wore black lace-up boots, and her head extended above the doorway. 'DON'T TAAACH!' she boomed as I dragged my fingernails along the wall to gather some of the ancient paint.

I blushed and straightened my headband.

How *very* horrid.

I tried to look offended in the hope that she might take pity. Maybe even fancy me. Let me into her circle of giant people's trust. I pouted and did fish face lips. Opened my eyes wide like that actress in the Charlie Chaplin movies who never talks but constantly appears shocked. But when I caught my reflection in the mirrored aviators of the guy standing next to me, I looked more like a stupefied camel with no teeth than a damsel in distress, so I gave up and went on my way. Making sure to lower my eyes and cover my breasts as I did so.

The inside of Menander House is beautiful.

Full of colourful frescoes and mosaics. The walls are covered with ancient artwork depicting scenes of war and love. Intricate details shaded with dark red and gold, worn away by years of air. I twirled around, reminding myself that thousands of years ago this was someone's home—a room where women in white dresses and men in leather sandals were served platters of olives and figs.

Snap! Suddenly there were voices. Foreign-sounding female voices. Breaking the magic and the tranquillity.

'Beautiful Yah? A true depiction of the scene. Yada, yada, yada'.

'Yah, yah, yah, and the interesting thing about this is that the shades reflect the … yah, yah, yah'.

My eyes fell to the corner of the atrium where a group of students sat on the dusty tiled floor, talking amongst themselves. Loudly. Artists, surrounded by charcoal and pencils. Five women in their early twenties, each wearing smocks and Doc Martens and silver rings on their thumbs. Huddled together, away from the crowd, looking relaxed and young. Sketching on expensive-looking paper.

Sharing an orange.

Whenever you go to an arty city, no matter where it is, you will always find a group like this. The unconventional backpackers. Travelling the globe in the name of art. Staying in communes and talking about minimalism and symbolism, and vegetarianism. They never differ. Or shave. And they're always as skinny as rakes because all they ever eat is effing oranges.

With my pride still stinging from being publicly humiliated by Giganti the Gatekeeper, I scowled bitterly in the direction of the young, carefree girls. Berated them with my eyes. Not all of us had time to sit and doodle the day away. They needed to keep their voices down.

This was a morgue, not a playground.

One of the girls looked my way and muttered something under her breath. An eruption of giggles followed.

How rude.

I knew what they were up to—laughing at my headband—mocking me. I was in two minds to walk over and grind my foot into their drawings. Smudge their wispy charcoal sketches with my callusy heel. But I was scared that mighty Gustav might see me and force me to do dirty things with her out the back, so I remained where I was and leaned provocatively against the wall.

Humph. Laughing at me, are you girls?

My eyes narrowed. I'll show them how a real woman behaves.

With one leg bent and shoulders pulled back, I reached into my day bag and pulled out a warm, overripe banana—the one I'd put in there two days ago. Seductively, moodily, *artily,* I peeled the skin from the fruit. Wetting my lips and guiding the bruised bulbous end into my mouth. Never once taking my eyes off the group. The girls looked uncomfortable. Disturbed. Violated. Uneasily they buried their faces in their work and continued to sketch.

Ha! Suck on that, you veggie mutants.

I smacked my lips together triumphantly—one nil to me.

'Hey, laydee!' came the thunderous voice. 'NO EAT IN HERE !' Igor, the security guard. Casting me in darkness with her colossal knockers.

Choosing to ignore the fact that the room reeked of oranges.

The only reason my kids agreed to come to Pompeii was that I told them they'd get to see dead bodies.

'Is that it?' blurted Sonny as we stood behind the glass of Exhibit No 32 and peered at what looked like a heap of sun-baked clay. I'll admit, it was a bit shit. Not a speck of withered flesh to be seen. No dried corpses with hairless skulls and skeleton fingers. Nothing. Just a bunch of clay mannequins.

I was annoyed.

I had wanted this to be a tender moment for everyone. I'd pre-empted my reaction on seeing the grisly remains of men, women, and children—skeletons with grotesquely long nails. I'd planned to use this opportunity as a homeschooling lesson. Explain to my children that when humans die, their nails still grow.

That kind of knowledge is what ensures a student's entrance into Oxford.

But this exhibit was rubbish. The bodies looked like oversized versions of Morph. I half expected Tony Hart to jump out from behind the glass and splat us with a load of blue paint. (*If you've never heard of Take Hart, Google it. It's brill.*) Still, regardless of the anti-climax, I went on with my plan. I stood up straight and closed my eyes.

'Terrible, isn't it?' I bleated in my best "A" level drama acting voice. 'Those poor, innocent victims. And that boy. Buried in time. His only crime was to carry a loaf of bread home to his mother'.

If I say so myself, the monologue was touching.

But when I opened my eyes, my family was gone—deserted me. Sonny was walking into the distance, looking back and shaking his head as if to say, *don't ever tell anyone that we're related,* and Brian and Tessa were over by the toilets playing that game where you trace a word with your finger on the other's back, and then try and guess what it says.

I was about to turn and follow them when all of a sudden, I heard a noise.

Whispering and giggling.

Not the ghosts of Pompeiians gone by. No. The arty backpackers. The new-age orange-suckers. My tormentors. Standing to the left of me.

I turned to face them. Resisting the urge to pull on my mole whisker.

One of the girls was tapping a pencil casually against her closed mouth. She lowered it and blew her blunt scissored fringe from her eyes. In her hand was a fresh piece of artwork—an abstract drawing on a sheet of expensive No 12 weighted guild paper. Unashamedly, I feasted my eyes upon it.

The sketch was good. I'll give her that. Albeit dark and impressionistic, it accurately represented what stood before her. An angular glass cage depicting death and destruction. A lonely, twisted figure—a woman wearing a very nice headband, kneeling to face the glass. Her face contorted with grief and sorrow.

And wait. There was something else. What was that?

I squinted at the sheet of paper. Focused my vision. There, on the floor beside the sketched woman, was an object. Drawn in the shape of a crescent. Rotten. Half-eaten and filled with tiny maggots.

I took a step forward to get a closer look. *Was that a …? Could it be my …?* It was. It bloody well was. The banana. They had drawn the fucking banana.

Well, well, well. How very avant-garde.

CHAPTER FOURTEEN
ENGLAND

We went to a festival last night. A Rock Fest. I got to stay up late past ten o'clock. I'm writing this diary entry with a bit of a hangover, actually. I know this will shock you, me being the classy, organic chick I am. But what can I say? Sometimes even *this* mummy has to let her hair down. Chill a little. Go a bit wild.

We are in Tavistock, a thriving market town in West Devon, England.

Tavistock (or Tavy as the locals call it) lies on the western edge of Dartmoor National Park—about fifteen miles north of Plymouth. Tavy is a very pretty town. It has a weir, which is lit at night, a beautiful park with ancient oak trees, and a Benedictine Abbey where a bunch of hungry monks invented the Devonshire Cream Tea.

Tavy has also been named the best place to live in Britain by the *Sunday Times*. I know. Quite the accolade.

I have to say; I'm not sure I agree.

I mean, it's pretty and quaint and lovely, and yes, there's a nice little pannier market that sells loads of good stuff, but the best place in Britain to live? I don't think so.

There are far too many pasty shops for my liking. And the charity shops are way too overpriced. This is probably because everyone who lives in Tavistock is posh, and rather than admit that their once-new V-neck sweater is now an old bally second-hand piece of shit, they refer to it as vintage. And then price it accordingly. *So annoying.*

Anyway.

How can Tavy be Blighty's best place to live when there's never anywhere to park your car when you go to the shops? Nowhere. Not unless you're willing to be in and out in less than sixty minutes. It's a nightmare. You spend half your day circling the one-way system like a hawk. Eyeing up the dizzy bays with envy. Wishing you had a blue badge.

And it's not even as if you can think about walking; because you can't. The cobbled streets in Tavy are so bloody steep and cobbly that you'd need a pair of those Forest Gump-style metal braces stuck to your legs to keep you upright.

So.

If you decide to visit Tavistock (and with this glowing review in front of you, why wouldn't you?), I suggest you take advantage of the excellent bus service. That way, you won't break your ankle carrying your pasties up the hill, *and* you can pretend you're doing it to save the planet. Which always goes down well. Especially in la-di-da places like Tavistock.

On a more positive note (hurray!), Tavistock is renowned for hosting tribute bands. Lookalikes. Men and women who dress up as their idols and sing their songs. Tavy's social calendar heaves with these groups. The Bootleg Beatles, Oasisn't, Diana Froth. AC/DShe. They're all here.

To be honest with you, I've never been keen on tribute bands. I always thought they were a bit sad. I mean, who wants to watch a wannabe rock star dress up in his mother's nightie and sing "I Want to Break Free" into a vacuum cleaner?

But since visiting England, my mind has changed towards lookalikes.

Changed big time.

We had never been to a proper music festival. One with sex and drugs, and body fluids. While in the throes of planning this world trip, when euphoric, random promises were being thrown around in an attempt to make everything sound good, I told the kids that when we visited England, we'd go to the Glastonbury Festival. Spend at least three days there.

Complete fib.

Everyone knows that tickets to the Glastonbury Festival are at least three hundred quid each. Only a bunch of basket-weaving morons would pay that much to stand in the middle of a field with mud smeared all over their naked bodies, miles from the action and freezing their droopy bits off.

No. Not for us. Glastonbury Festival wouldn't be seeing a penny of my family's money, thank you very much. Not a dime.

But all was not lost.

As luck would have it, Tavistock was hosting a festival of its own. And it fell on the weekend of our stay. *Ideal!* This local event was to be held on the community college sports field across the road from Morrisons supermarket. The gates opened at 10.00 a.m., and the party was to continue late into the night. All money raised would go to local charities.

Brightly coloured posters plastered on lamp posts around the town promoted the extravaganza with pride. "SATURDAY NIGHT IS TAVIFEST! Face painting! Pulled pork baps. Beer tent! UK's BEST tribute bands! FREE to all!"

Sadly, one of the posters had been vandalised (the one in the ladies' public toilet next to the post office). Some little shit had crossed out "Tavy" and replaced it with the word "wank." Scribbled over it in red marker. So now it read: "SATURDAY NIGHT IS WANKFEST!"

I smiled when I read it. *What luck!*

Not only were we going to a festival, but bad boys would be attending. Hooligans. Yobos.

This would prove to the kids what a dirty rock n' roller their mother really was. I could see it now. Brian and me drinking and dancing and twirling. Like those far-out parents who get high with their kids and call them hun and babe.

I might even convince Brian to take his socks off.

It was Friday. The day before the festival. The four of us sat on the wall outside the communal swimming pool. Eating pasties.

'Guess where we're going tomorrow?' I said in the same voice mothers use with their toddlers on Christmas Eve. Sonny fished out a piece of turnip from the inside of his pasty and inspected the findings. 'We … are … going to a music festival!' I nodded wildly and held open my hands, waiting for the flood of enthusiasm and thanks.

The pasty plopped into the bottom of the paper bag.

'Seriously?' said Sonny, his interest suddenly piqued. 'What? A real one? With weed and stuff?'

I shifted uncomfortably. No mother wants to admit that their son might be a closet junkie.

'Kind of', I lied. 'Only it's more of a local music festival. Like a rock concert for families. And it's all in aid of charity'.

Christ almighty Liz, try a bit harder. It sounds kak.

I crossed my legs and pressed on. 'There'll be thousands of people there. It'll probably go on to at least three or four'. (I left out the 'in the afternoon' part.)

I casually bit the nobbily bit from the end of the pasty. Brian shot me a look of warning.

Sonny narrowed his eyes in suspicion.

'Is it free?'

It was the morning of the festival. Because I am resourceful and have a severe addiction to alcohol, I instructed Brian to nip out to Lidl's and buy two bottles of red wine—under a fiver, mind.

'That way, we won't have to spend money at the bar'.

I smirked at my cleverness. I knew how these "free" festivals made their money. No one would take me for a mug.

Carefully, I wrapped the bottles in a tea towel and buried them in the bottom of my reusable hessian shopping bag. I was excited. Very excited. The last time I was at a live music concert was when I saw Wham at the Cornwall Coliseum in 1984. I had hung over the railings wearing my "Choose Life" tee-shirt. Screaming at George to feel me up or snog me.

Silly me. Little did I know George only had eyes for Andrew.

It was a dull, overcast day, and the ground was slightly damp. A silver-haired man on a Zimmer frame met us at the festival entrance, welcoming us into the large canvas gazebo that was there to provide shelter for the organisers.

'Morning, team!' he beamed cheerfully, reaching over and patting Tessa on the head like a prize poodle. 'Ready to have some fun, are we?'

He took a paper hankie from the pocket of his hi-vis reflective jacket and dabbed at his watery blue eyes focused on the donation box beside him.

Daft old fool.

I was tempted to shove his head into the hessian bag and show him the wine I had stashed. Bellow into his hearing aid, 'Don't think you'll be making any money out of me at your rip-off charity bar, fella!'

But I didn't.

It's not nice to abuse geriatrics. Especially not at charity events. Instead, I smiled politely and said, 'That's a very nice fluorescent coat you're wearing, sir. Are you a real policeman?' Then I popped fifty pence into his box and moved nicely along to where two women volunteers with arthritic fingers were sitting behind a trestle table— giving away woollen pansy brooches. Pink ones they'd crocheted themselves.

'Would you like one, my love?' asked the lady on the right, pushing the box towards me.

'Super. How nice. Thank you'. I took two. One for me and one for my mum. She had explicitly asked that I bring her a gift from our travels. Something "typically English".

Leaving the gazebo behind us, we walked out onto the festival field.

Ta-da!!

Sonny stopped in his tracks. His mouth fell open. 'I thought you said this was a proper festival. With whistles and music and stuff?' He squinted out into the empty grassland beyond. 'Why is there a Mister Whippy van here?'

The place was deserted. Deathly. Nothing but a couple of rubbish-looking food stalls, a beer tent, and a line of PAL Hire portaloos.

A group of pensioners had claimed the grass in front of the makeshift stage with their upright chairs and were busy building a protective village-of-the-dammed-like circle with their blue and white cool boxes.

'I'm sure it'll get busy late on', I chirped. 'When the bands kick off'.

I pinned the crocheted brooch onto my flowy top and skipped to the tea tent to ask for a paper cup.

As the day wore on more and more people began to arrive. Groups of teenagers. Families. Nanas and grandads—brought along to keep watch over boisterous grandchildren so their knackered parents could escape and get sloshed. There was a local newspaper editor snapping random pictures. A big gang of blokes dressed up as saucy chambermaids (obviously a stag do), a dog-walking group in green waxed jackets and wellies to match, and a few lone vegetarians.

Displaying their unhappiness outside the pulled pig stand. Demanding to know why there weren't any plant-based options or kombucha.

By five o'clock, the place was buzzing.

It was marvellous. A couple of big bass speakers boomed out songs from the 'Now That's What I Call Music' album while groups of friends gathered and swayed, enjoying the aroma of fried onions, dried mud, and stale beer.

England at its finest.

At half past six, an announcement came over the tannoy. 'Listen up, folks!' crackled a male voice with a heavy Devonshire accent. 'In thirty minutes, the tribute bands will commence. So let your hair down, get your dancing shoes on and get ready to party like it's 1999! Let's show 'em how it's done, TAVY!!'

A cheer went up. The butterflies in my stomach fluttered. *How exciting! How trippy and kicky and cool.*

Having consumed copious amounts of milky tea and masses of complimentary stale ginger biscuits, I decided that now would be the perfect time to start on the good stuff—warm my cockles. Crack open the vino.

I scanned the field for the kids—all clear. Nowhere to be seen. *Excellent.* The last thing I wanted was for them to witness their mother behaving like one of those dirty hobos I had warned them about in New York.

Leaving Brian standing next to the tombola talking to some boring old fuddy-duddy about regenerative farming, I headed towards the portaloos with my hessian bag and discreetly poured the dark red wine into a tripled-up paper cup.

Swig. Gulp. Ahh.

The first mouthful is always the best.

I closed my eyes and smacked my lips together loudly. I was ready. Raring to go. I scurried back to the action, hugging the edge of the field inconspicuously. Catlike. Shadowy. A dangerous punk. Like Eddie Van Halen or Amy Winehouse. Or maybe the sewer rat from *Flushed Away*.

I have three fundamental dance moves. All very sexy.

Depending on my mood and the beat of the music, I alternate the moves accordingly.

Dance move number one is where I use both hands and shoulders to imitate a rabbit burrowing through a tunnel. At the same time (and this is the crucial part), I bite my bottom lip. Resembling someone with an exaggerated overbite in terrible pain. This move is probably my hottest. I often see Brian looking at me with utter longing when the teeth dance comes out.

The second is a little more modern. I like to use this move to show Tessa that I'm a free-spirited flower chick. A boho babe who can dance like Sandie Shaw.

Standing with my feet glued to the floor, I move only from my knees. Ignoring the fact that I resemble one of those blow-up wind-man signs you see outside car showrooms. I pair this with a freaky thing that I do with my fingers. Like I'm untangling two invisible wigs. I reckon it looks psychedelic, but I'm still perfecting the technique. The last time I performed these moves, I was asked if I was studying sign language.

And lastly, move number three. The choo-choo train.

This move sees me impersonating Thomas the Tank Engine. Only I do it with a sexy "come and get me, Gordon" look in my eye. I'll admit. I don't use this one often. It's quite grotesque. Terrifying actually.

With Brian (still) stuck to the side of the farmer's hip and the kids nowhere to be seen (probably drinking the blue dye out of the portaloos with some roughnecks), I decided to enjoy the music alone. Pushing a couple of old biddies sideways, I made my way to the front of the stage, where I rested my elbows on the wooden raised platform and drummed my fingers on an imaginary keyboard—running my hands from side to side.

How cool I must look.

The first act on stage was the Neil Diamond tribute act: 'I Am a Diamond'.

Brilliant he was.

Strutting around on the stage in his platform shoes, wearing silky pants and a slightly too-small waistcoat. I like a man in a black wig. Especially when he keeps looking over at me and winking. Teasing me. Inviting me to chew on a bit of his crackling rose.

'Haaands, touching haaands … Reaching out, touching me, touching YOU! Sweeet Caroliinne …'

I stomped my feet down hard three times to the beat and cheered wholeheartedly, not caring that Neil-not-Neil was slightly off-key and his pants were too tight. Nothing wrong with a rough-cut stone. I sang along in my loudest voice and did that thing where you make a heart with your thumbs and first fingers, holding it up in the air so that Neil-not-Neil would know that I loved him and everyone behind me would see that I was bang up-to-date with concert etiquette.

Three support acts later and already two-thirds through my second bottle of wine, I decided to visit the ladies.

Coming out of the portaloos, I bumped into my daughter chattering and laughing with a bunch of new pals. 'Oops. Sorry, hunz. Scuuuzze me'. I stood aside, burping and giggling. Hoping that I looked like Elizabeth Taylor in her tipsy years and not like the old slag who ran the pub in *Les Misérables*.

Tessa eyed me and my bag with suspicion. She didn't like it when I was away from her father for too long. 'What are you doing? Why aren't you with Daddy?'

She stepped towards me. I backed away.

Cocking my head and looking out from under my fringe like a fragile Lady Di when she was interviewed for *Panorama*.

Tessa looked confused. I had a sudden urge to take her in my arms and rock her like a baby. But then I remembered that she was fourteen.

Years not months.

'Why don't you go home? I will be *fine* here', she pressed, moving away from the circle of shadows and whispering in a low, desperate tone. 'I've made some new friends. You could go home and do that meditation thing you always do in bed'.

Pssht. As if. Little madam. Telling me what to do. Treating me like an idiot. I don't think so.

I squinted over my daughter's shoulder at the new bosom buddies. Narrowing my eyes and feigning sobriety. One was wearing a long black trench coat and had a myriad of piercings. Another, navy blue lips and one eyebrow. And the little one at the front—the one with orange hair? *Jesus Christ.* It was a cross between a gremlin and Beaker from the Muppets.

I opened my mouth to speak. 'Remember that Stephen Spielberg fil—'

'Please, Mummy. Just go home'.

I let out a deep sigh and quickly weighed up my options.

Let me think. Go home with Brian, knowing that three minutes after hitting the hay, we would be snoring like pigs and twitching like two half-dead rabbits OR stay at Tavifest and get pissed even more. I opted for the latter.

'No, thank you, sweetheart', I said in my skipsy, tipsy festival voice. 'The main act is coming on soon. Mummy's staying. And she'll be dancing at the front of the stage regardless of what you or Daddy thinks'. Then I turned to leave with my nose in the air. Holding tight to my hessian bag and my blue raffle ticket. Trying my hardest to walk in a straight line.

'Faaack. What's wrong with your mum? She is *so* passive-aggressive maaan', a voice said from behind.

'Oh … you know …. It's mostly her hormones. She just acts a bit weird sometimes'.

The highlight of the festival, the star turn if you like, was Grey Blabbath. A semi-professional rock band brought in from London. Paid for by Tavy Chamber of Commerce. They were due on stage at ten o'clock but, in true rock and roll fashion, were late.

How reckless. How wild.

The organisers panicked. "Now That's What I Call Music" filled the speakers once more.

At ten past ten, Grey Blabbath's vehicle sped up onto the grass alongside the stage, etching skid marks in the turf. I locked eyes with the old codger whose job was to walk around the field with a big torch. We both shook our heads. *Very un-called for. Such bad manners.* Nobody likes to get mud on their crepe soles. Especially not at a concert.

Grooving half-heartedly to the CD while guarding my place at the front of the stage, I watched in secret admiration as the members of Grey Blabbath piled out of their white transit van. Frowning and angry. Giving off fucking-late-as-usual vibes. Shrouded in a cloud of vape fumes. Dangerous. Like Guns and Roses, only cockney.

There were three of them in total: a woman and two men. The woman was gorgeous and rock-chicky. Skin-tight black pants, studded belt around her teeny, tiny waist, and a *sleeveless* purple vest showing off her perfectly contoured triceps.

Dangerous rock chicks always wear purple.

I cursed myself for not donning my new purple neckerchief. The one with the printed oak leaves and little dog bones that I bought from the National Trust shop in the sale last week.

I followed the beauty's gaze as she scanned the half-empty field. Her black eyelinered eyes rested on me. I blushed. The look on her face said it all. *You have to be kidding me? All the way down the M4 in the back of a van, and the only person here is some weird alkie wearing a crocheted flower dancing like C3PO?'*

Ten minutes later, Grey Blabbath came to the stage.

Swaggering.

Not even apologising for their lateness.

I watched as the female lead singer ran her hands up and down the microphone lead provocatively. Winking suggestively at the bare-chested peroxide-blonde guitarist.

They must be lovers.

My, my.

A prickly sweat covered my body.

How erotic. How kinky. A real-life Sid Vicious and Nancy Spungen. Right here in Tavy.

I peered back over at Brian. He was standing in the same spot with his hand on his chin. Chuckling and nodding in agreement with the farmer wearing green wellies. My eyes returned to Sid. Sid, the guitarist. Sid with a huge ball and chain tattooed around his neck. Steamy, saucy, sexy Sid.

I know what you're thinking.

You're thinking I fancied him. And you'd be right. *Bang on.* I found the overpowering smell of patchouli oil and raspberry vape so attractive that whenever Sid shouted, 'Are you hearing us out front, Tavifest?' I came over all frisky. Kept putting two thumbs up in the air and yelling, 'Yeeesss!! We can hear you loud and clear, captain'.

And yes. I actually said: *Captain.* I know. Toe-curling.

Oh, how I danced and boogied. All night long, I was on my feet. Standing at the front and using all my moves. Trying to get Nancy's attention so she'd think, *wow! Where did that chick learn to dance like a train? We'd better ask her for a threesome, Sid.*

I even managed to get Sonny to dance with me. 'Get into the groove, BABE', I blurted into his face with my red-wine breath, yanking at his arm and standing on his toe.

'When are we going?' he bellowed over the music, trying hard to ignore my wig-untangling psychedelic finger moves and the fact that I kept blinking at Sid.

'Who said anything about going?' I sang out happily. 'Let's stay here for e-v-e-r!'

Then I held my arms out wide. Whizzing and twirling around like a spinning top. Outstretched bat-winged arms, revolving round and round, looking at the sky and laughing. Neurotically.

How fabulous I must look!

Like Kate Bush in 'Wuthering Heights'. Bonnie Tyler in 'Total Eclipse'. Or maybe even Jimmy Summerville in 'You Are My World'. Only taller. And without the Glaswegian accent.

Tavistock is a market town. It lies on the western edge of Dartmoor National Park—about fifteen miles north of Plymouth. It has a weir, which is lit at night, a beautiful park with ancient oak trees, and a Benedictine Abbey where a bunch of hungry monks invented the Devonshire Cream Tea.

And it is, officially, without a doubt, THE best place in Britain to live. No question about it.

Even if it does have shit parking.

CHAPTER FIFTEEN
THE LAST STOP

It was the final leg of our journey. The last stop. We were back in Thailand.

We all loved it so much the first time, we decided to return.

Life in Thailand is easy. The food is delicious, the weather is warm, and the people are kind. It is also incredibly cheap. Rather than spend the time travelling around the country, we chose to stay and explore the capital city, Bangkok.

Our flight back to New Zealand was the next day.

I'd always dreamed of going to Bangkok. Ever since watching Nicole Kidman sweat it out in a prison cell wearing nothing but a grey tank top and frizzy orange hair. *One day*, I told myself, *I'll go to Thailand and be just like her.*

Only without the heroin and the thirty-year impoundment sentence.

Bangkok conjures up images of danger and intrigue. When you tell people you are taking your teenagers to Bangkok, you feel plucky and hip. Brave and young. Like a free-flowing menstrual cup user who drives a hand-painted combi and knows everything there is to know about bongs.

But Bangkok does not feel dangerous. Not in the slightest. The city is patient and hazy, warm and romantic. And tampons are sold in most pharmacies.

Bangkok is best at night when the sun sets, and long shadows are thrown over the pavements, silhouetting the skyscrapers against the navy blue sky. Beautiful, chaotic Bangkok, with its masses of mumble jumble power lines strung carelessly across random buildings.

Bangkok, with its market stalls manned by owners who sit on white plastic stools, chatting softly and rapidly into their phones. Unphased by the fact that there are no customers to buy the live frogs that writhe around in buckets at their feet.

We'd been in Bangkok for five days.

We'd indulged in street food, visited the gigantic sleeping Buddha, and walked across the Rama VIII Bridge at midnight. We'd even managed to squeeze in a little Bangkok education at breakfast.

'Mummy?' Tessa asked, popping the bubbles in her milkshake with a paper straw. 'Why is it called Bangkok? I mean, it's a bit weird, isn't it? Bang *(waits for three seconds and fiddles with the straw some more)* kok'. She smirked at her brother. I stuck out my chin.

Pfft. She must think I came in on a Thai gravy boat.

I wanted to tell her that the name Bangkok came from an old Buddha who had bashed his pecker against a willow tree, but Brian said that was untrue and that I shouldn't fill the kid's heads with shite, especially since I was in charge of their education. So I regurgitated what I'd had read on some website: 'Bang: meaning village or district. Makok: meaning wild plums'.

Bangkok. The village of wild plums. Genius.

Tessa stifled a yawn and examined her split ends. *Damn it. I knew I should have gone with the bruised knob story.*

It was the last night of our trip, and because I am thoughtful and kind and only ever think of other people, I thought it would be grand to treat us all to a massage. An end-of-trip celebration.

I know. My cup spilleth over.

I'd always wanted to get a Thai massage. Not one of those where a big fat man in tiny red underpants throws you on the floor and stamps on your head. A soft one. A gentle one. One that starts at the toes and ends at the knees.

I read somewhere that having your feet rubbed tenderly gives you inner holistic energy and makes you a much nicer parent who is really good at cooking.

I ran my finger around the rim of my coffee cup. 'Who wants to get a foot massage?' I asked casually, as if it was a regular habit of mine to offer recreational fun and paid-for activities to my culture-starved children.

Tessa's eyebrows left her forehead. 'What? A real one? With massage oil and stuff? Not a fish tank one?'

Simpleton.

She was referring to the last time we were in Thailand. When I'd paid a hefty amount of dosh for us all to stick our feet into a grotty fish tank and watch as baby piranhas gobbled the flesh from between our toes. It had earned me twelve likes on Facebook but had given the child nightmares for weeks. Honestly, sometimes I don't know why I bother.

'No', I sniffed. 'Not a fishy one. A real one. From a massage parlour on Khoa San Road'.

Sonny put down his phone.

'I'll do it', he said, drumming his fingers on the table and jigging his knees frenziedly like one of those druggies at the chemist who come in for their prescription fix because they are trying to get clean and wean themselves off meth.

Christ. I might have just discovered the cure to nomophobia.

After making a song and dance about the dent that this massage would make in our remaining budget and how I expected everyone to be extremely grateful and remain in debt to me for the next ten years, we set off for Khoa San Road.

The best way to get to Khoa San Road (from any of the suburbs in Bangkok) is to take a riverboat. Several boats run up and down the Chao Phraya River, but the commuter boat is the one to go for. Yes, there are crowds of people, and yes, the little man in charge screams at you like Rumpelstiltskin if you don't get on board fast enough, but that's part of the fun. And anyway, it's the cheapest, and that's all that counts.

You'll know when you hit Khoa San Road. You'll just know.

Your nostrils will fill, and your eyes will feast. You will feel giddy and curious. Plucky and (unless you are under twenty-five) slightly sleazy. You'll linger on the pavements and try not to stare. Breathe in the smell of stale alcohol and smoky street food. You'll marvel at the brightly coloured oranges piled up next to fresh juice stalls and thumb through racks of vibrant sarongs that only ever come in one size and, no matter which way you tie them, always make your hips look massive and huge.

Khoa San Road is filled with bars and market stalls, and massage parlours. Beautiful women with big hands and prominent Adam's apples stride confidently along the strip. Jewellery shops offer discounts on international shipping, and street hawkers try their hardest to flog you a fried tarantula with a stick rammed up its backside.

'Ohhh, Mummy! Shall we buy one?' Tessa said, playfully pulling at my sleeve. 'So I can take a photo for Snapchat?'

I picked up the pace and narrowed my eyes like a pygmy shrew.

Everyone knows that eating tarantulas is a tourist gimmick. No Thai person in their right mind would buy a spider off the street. Not when there are perfectly decent 7-Elevens on every corner.

'Maybe later', I said. 'We'll see'.

Flanked by two noisy bars boasting neon lights and pink plastic palm trees, the massage shop was in the centre of the bustling thoroughfare. A glass-fronted building with rows of padded reclining chairs arranged alongside the pavement set up for exhibitionists who preferred to take their massage in full view of the passing public rather than retreat inside to a more private space.

I went to work, claiming four chairs in the front row.

There was no way I was missing an opportunity like this. What better way to look cool on the socials than to be seen getting your trotters massaged on the streets of Bangkok? I'd make sure to use a hashtag that would bring me plenty of views. #bangkokpleasure.

Yes. That should do it.

'Oh, my God. Can we not?' said Sonny, withering with embarrassment. He stood with his back to the shop; his hands rammed deep into the pockets of his shorts. Drooping. A young orange-tanned woman wearing a short white skirt and long glittery eyelashes hopped along the street in front of him. Adjusting the back strap of her shoe. She caught Sonny's eye and gave him a tipsy wave before falling onto her friends and exploding into a fit of giggles.

'I'm serious', he snapped. 'Let's just go in. It's boiling out here'.

Poor boy.

His bright purple cheeks sent a surge of pity through my veins. Not only was this mature (but still definitely very much pubescent) young lad about to get his toes stroked by an undercover sex worker, but his mother was insisting that he do it in public. While sitting next to his dad, who was wearing his reading glasses and that repulsive tee-shirt that was so thin you could see his for-some-reason-constantly-erect nipples.

We went inside.

An elderly lady manned the door. She was in her late nineties, at least. The Madam. With beady eyes and bony hands.

'Sawadee ka', I beamed, making sure to use my loudest voice so those around me would know I was bilingual. 'Foot massage? Discount for four?'

The lines on the woman's face deepened. She coughed into a tissue before rattling something off in Thai to the girl standing beside her.

'My mother no speak English. One-hour massage four people, two hundred baht. Each person. No discount'.

Tight old bag.

We paid our baht and were shown to a bench where we were told to take off our shoes and slip our feet into a pair of white towelling slippers. The look of horror on Madam's face, when she clocked the colour of my heels, was pleasing.

Ha! Too late to double the price now, old girl. Best get crackin'.

Slippered up and ready to go, we entered into a small, dimly lit room.

The walls were painted deep maroon. Dark velvet drapes covered a bricked-up window, and the smell of cheap incense was overpowering.

Tessa whimpered. Brian took her hand.

I looked around. Unable to decide if I had brought my family to a Thai opium den or Mystic Meg's fortune-telling chamber. It didn't matter. All that was important was the cost. This massage had set us back eight hundred big ones. Everyone had better bloody well enjoy it. Poppy seed drugs or not.

Madam backed out of the room slowly and smoothly like one of those retired volunteers who push the food trolly around hospital wards and never stop long enough for you to choose a decent sandwich.

'You. Wait', she said. Then closed the door and left.

Within seconds, four Thai women filed out from behind a curtain. Smiling like *Miss World* contestants. They signalled for us to sit on the chairs along the room's back wall, then bowed robotically and knelt at our feet.

I looked at Sonny. He was crimson. The heat from his cheeks must have added fifty degrees to the room's temperature. 'Unbutton your shirt', I mouthed, gesturing wildly to his chest. He pretended not to see me and glued his eyes to the price pamphlet he'd brought from the front desk.

I wanted to say, 'Jesus didn't read a pamphlet when Mary Magdalene washed his feet did he?' But I thought that might embarrass him and get him all worked up about religion, so I sat back against the wall and rolled my eyes up in my head, hoping that I looked wise and sensual and not like Helen Keller in pain.

Carefully, our feet were lifted and placed into round clay bowls filled with luscious warm water.

The massage ladies swirled water around our toes and ankles. *Lovely*. Very nice, indeed.

Tessa's attendant was young and smiling. She admired my daughter's light pink ankles with her beautiful almond-shaped eyes and patted her flesh gently.

My woman kept blowing air out of her open mouth, frowning and tutting. Her breath smelled of stale cigarettes, and she pressed down really hard on my heels with her thumbs in an attempt to remove the stubborn grime. I wanted to ask her what the Thai word was for "Brillo Pad".

I looked over at Brian. He seemed tense. Frigid.

He had both hands on his knees as if ready to bolt at any given opportunity.

'Relax, my love ....' I wanted to soothe, 'the solar plexus is the gateway to your sexuality. Sit back and feel the eroticism. Observe your wife having her feet bathed by another woman ....'

I waited until he was watching, then I licked my index finger and began running it up and down my neck. Then I smiled my special smile.

Brian's eyes widened. He looked petrified.

He began picking bits of imaginary fluff from his shorts and unrolling and rolling his socks into a ball. Neatly and pedantically. Ensuring that the embossed smiley faces on the ribbed top lined up perfectly.

Green leaves floated in the water of the foot bowls. Whether it was mint or bits of iceberg lettuce, I couldn't say, but whatever it was, the slimy particles kept getting caught between my toes, and it felt gross.

I wanted to flick my foot out and discard them. Boot them off.

But I refrained.

No Thai lady deserves to have soggy vegetable peelings hurled between her pencilled eyebrows. Not when she's on her knees working.

Once the water had turned cold and was a dark brown colour, our feet were lifted out and placed onto the lap of the masseur to be dried. The towels felt crispy and crusty, as though they'd been left outside on the line for too long. I wanted to suggest a bit of fabric conditioner wouldn't go amiss, especially for two hundred baht a pop, but I held my tongue.

The masseur smiled and rubbed the material around my feet. 'Feel good?' she asked, not waiting for an answer.

It felt like a stale Ryvita being rammed between the soft flesh of my toes. It was awful. Revolting. The most excruciatingly hideous sensation I'd ever experienced. I hated it.

'Thank you', I said. 'That feels wonderfully nice'.

The lady pushed my trousers above my knee. I smiled at Brian. He blinked. It had been months since he'd clapped his eyes on any part of my body above the ankle. And time had been cruel. Gone were the knobbly bones of youth, and in their place, a pair of bloated dimply navel oranges.

The masseuse set her jaw and began pounding at a raised vein on the back of my calf, moving her hands swiftly from leg to foot. I prodded my toes into her little palms and reminded myself that it is the personality that counts, not how skinny your knees are.

If anyone ever tells you that a Thai foot massage is relaxing, don't believe them. They are lying. It's a big con.

Yes, there are silk cushions and ding-dong music playing from the ears of the gold Buddha ornaments, and yes, *at first,* the massage is relaxing. But thirty minutes into it, things get rough. Very rough. Do not be fooled by those women with sweet smiles and red-painted nails. They are sadistic torturers. Horrid and cruel. Their hands are stronger than pit shovels. Designed to crush and pummel every bit of stress from your feet and ankles.

They. Will. Hurt. You.

The remaining half-hour of our massage was like something out of a Stephen King novel. I kept waiting for my lady masseur to look up from between my toes and say: 'You've been a very dirty birdy, haven't you...? Let's see now...Where's my hammer?'

Pummel, punch, twist. Yank, squeeze, whack. Drrrrrrrdrrrdrrrrdrrrr chop suey hands up and down your shins just for the hell of it. Slap, bang, punch, another few punches, and then finally … Done.

Oh, no wait.

Whack. Drrrrdddd. One more pummelly punch for good measure. There. Finished.

The massage was over. We were free to leave. Battered. Exhausted. Traumatised.

Tessa's adolescent legs looked like two deformed twigs, and Sonny's eyes, fixated on the Facebook logo on the wall the entire hour, showed early signs of cataracts. Brian's shorts were picked to threads, and me? My toes resembled ten skinless pork sausages that had been run over by a steam roller.

An hour after we arrived, we left the building. Bidding goodbye to The Madam, who, despite serving thousands of British tourists in her establishment for well over ninety years, could still only manage to say 'No credit' in English.

'Well, that was … interesting', said Sonny, staggering out onto the street and blinking rapidly to entice moisture back into his eyes. 'So, then? Who fancies a tarantula?'

I will never forget how I felt that night. Out there on the pavement on our last night in Bangkok.

Our trip was at the end. Tomorrow it would be over.

As the four of us stood outside in the warm night air, firing impressions and comments at each other and giggling like schoolchildren about what had just happened, it hit me. Right there, and then it hit me. I remember stopping for a moment and catching my breath. This was it. This was the moment.

'Look at us', I wanted to say. *Just look at us.*

But I kept the words in my head, choosing instead to observe silently. There they were. My family. My Brian. My Sonny. My Tessa. The three human beings who filled my heart with so much love it hurt.

I took a breath and held it.

Wishing that this moment could last forever.

I remember thinking that I should make an announcement. Say something important. Meaningful. Like they do in films, when something sad comes to an end, and everyone hugs and cries, and John Williams begins to play. But there was no need. Our twinkly-eyed laughter said it all. We knew. We would always know. Forever and ever and longer than that.

We'd always know.

Brian and I slipped our arms around our children's waists, and the four of us walked in a line down Khoa San Road. I tried to step in time and do that dance that Dorothy does when she's walking along the Yellow Brick Road with her weird friends, but I got it wrong and almost fell down a storm drain and broke my neck.

'I think it's time to go home', I said, beaming because I am the tenderest mother on the planet, and my children would remember this moment for the rest of their lives and definitely tell their own kids how cool their grandma was when I was dead.

Then we all started laughing and crossed the road.

To begin our next journey.

Our journey

home.

Chapter Sixteen
Home

D o you want to know the most challenging thing about travelling the world with your family for a year?

The thing that no one warns you about when you pack your bags, set off into the horizon and skip along the runway to explore countries you've only ever seen in films and eat foods you never knew existed?

Let me tell you.

The hardest thing about upping and leaving your regular life to spend twelve glorious months, three hundred and sixty-five wonderful days, eight thousand, seven hundred and sixty fabulous hours, and five hundred twenty-five thousand six hundred amazing minutes together is this.

Coming home.

Returning to reality. Getting back on with it.

That's the thing that no one prepares you for.

Twelve months after bidding New Zealand goodbye, we returned. The plane touched down in Auckland on a warm, wet, foggy day. It was early December, and while everything was blooming and people buzzed around, happily making plans for their upcoming summer Christmas BBQ on the beach, I felt horribly flat. I'm not kidding. If you'd laid me and a pancake next to each other on the road and compared us both, I would have made the pancake look like one of those gigantic inflatable happy helium balloons.

Returning to reality after living a life of travel that you have fully immersed yourself into and loved every minute of leaves you feeling a bit cheated.

Like when you have a job you love, and you're just getting into it, but then the boss dies or, even worse, retires, and tells you that he's closing the business and your job is now obsolete.

Or when you find the perfect little Italian restaurant, hiding in one of the suburbs not far from where you live, and you start going there every Wednesday night with your partner. You love it. It's romantic. The menu is perfect, and the price is right. And for some reason, whenever you eat there, you always go home and have sex. But then one night, you turn up, and there's a sign on the door saying, "Closed. Shop for lease".

That's how I felt when I returned home from our epic world trip.

Just as I was getting into the swing of our new life, learning the ropes of being together twenty-four-seven and knowing when to hold my tongue about who gets to use the charger, it was time to come home.

And I wasn't ready.

Not then. Not yet. *Probably not ever.*

The twelve months we spent travelling the world as a family were the best of my life. Phenomenal. Absolutely brilliant. Heavenly.

And I didn't want it to be over.

Of course, not all of us felt the same. Tessa was more than ready to come back. While she enjoyed the adventures and challenges of the trip, she missed her friends and longed for the comfort and stability of home. Also, season three of *Stranger Things* was due to be released soon, and the iPad was broken.

'Only two more days to go!' she sang happily as we shopped for souvenirs during our last week in Thailand. 'Not including today, tomorrow, and the day of the flight, there's only two more days to go! Hurray!'

The calculator app was open on her phone, and she was working out how many minutes she had left—counting the seconds until she could finally go home. Literally—the seconds.

Her excitement narked me.

Why is she being like this? Why? Why wasn't she wallowing in her own sorrow like me? Begging me to buy a coconut shack on some far-flung Hawaiian island and homeschool her until she was thirty-two?

We could count shells and drink sea urchin juice for breakfast. It could all be so perfect. I could change. But no. Here she was, annoying me with her stupid calculator.

'Yes, but look on the bright side!' I said, forcing her phone out of my face and almost cracking the screen, 'At least we still have five days left. Hurray!'

I know. It takes practice to be evil, but I'm getting the hang of it. Slowly and surely.

We each reacted differently to coming home.

I didn't see Brian for a few hours when we got back. He ran to his shed faster than his legs would carry him, muttering something about battery chargers and the need to tighten the cam belt on the lawnmower. I have no idea what he was doing. I think he was hoovering out the downspouts with his electric toothbrush.

Of us all, it was Brian who needed his own space the most.

He had just completed the mammoth task of taking his family around the world. Keeping us all safe. Being the rock.

Brian, the mediator. The peacekeeper. The one we all turned to when there was a problem. The one we all relied on.

Brian. The love of my life. My Scouse plumber. With his never-ending supply of love and patience.

And his need to clean.

I learned a lot about Brian during our time away. Things that I might never have known otherwise. Like, what a clean freak he is. While I always knew he was partial to a bit of Mr Sheen on his windscreen, I never realised that his obsession was quite so extreme.

Whereas I sought out aromatherapy oils to rub into my temples whenever we arrived in a new country, Brian would head straight for the cleaning stall on the market: 'Bleach?' he'd ask the locals. 'You have bleach? Domestos? Ajax?'

I should have seen it coming. The warning signs were there from the start. On our wedding day, he asked his best man to sanitise his hands before handing over the ring.

Tessa was the happiest to be back.

Five minutes after being home, she morphed into Laurence Llewelyn-Bowen, arranging a vase with beautiful dead twigs and feathers and placing it in the corner of her room. After she had finished with that, she colour-coordinated the coat hangers in her wardrobe.

I'll repeat that in case you missed it the first time.

She colour-coordinated the coat hangers in her wardrobe.

I know—poor girl.

How many nights had she laid awake on a sleeper bus in India thinking, *when I get home, I'm going to have all my white coat hangers to the left and the pink ones to the right?*

Tessa. The thirteen-year-old who never really wanted to go around the world and sleep on strangers' couches but who did it anyway, without a fuss.

I was so proud of her.

My beautiful, brave, diplomatic girl. She learned many things while she was travelling. Her talents shone brightly. When we were in England, she bought a ukulele and taught herself to play. She wrote songs and filled them with brilliant lyrics.

I wouldn't be surprised if she went on to have a career in the music industry.

Either that or end up on one of those reality TV shows where problematic kids seek help to combat their obsessive coat-hanger disorders.

Sonny loved travelling, but he was happy to be home.

He flew into his room at the speed of light and wired up his big mega-sound system to his fancy lights. The ones that flash in time to the music. Then he stood and stared at the size of his bed for hours, shaking his head and saying, 'I can't believe I've got it all to myself'.

Travelling brought out the entrepreneur in Sonny. Whatever he was doing on that phone every day turned out to be useful. He would spend hours and hours making vlogs and cinematic videos, working both behind and in front of the camera. He returned to New Zealand with a handful of skills and a headful of ideas. More determined than ever to create content and make his millions online.

Which is just as well. Because he still owes his dad nineteen dollars for the selfie stick he bought in India.

And finally, there's me. Liz.

The first few days back were a bit of a blur.

I remember everything feeling vaguely familiar but alien at the same time. It was almost as if I needed someone to tell me what to do next. How to live. Remind me of how things worked.

I kept expecting Eamonn Andrews to pop his head around the front door and present me with the big red book. 'Mother of two and wife of Brian! This is your life! The one you had before you left everything behind and pissed off around the world for a year'.

Only he wouldn't say 'pissed'. He'd say 'fecked' because he was Irish.

I swung from feeling sad that the trip was over to ecstatic it had happened. I couldn't believe that we'd done it. I still can't. We travelled the world with our kids for a year, and not only that, but we managed to do it for little more than the price of a new car.

I had fulfilled a dream burning inside me for many years. And that dream turned out to be a fairy tale.

Better than I could have ever imagined.

It wasn't long before I returned to my old self and felt on top of my game. Planning new adventures and reminding myself that we lived in New Zealand. A country that is open and spacious, and green. Where the people are friendly and say, 'Go for it!' when you tell them your plans to do something slightly out of the box and mental.

*If I were the prime minister of New Zealand (or was asked to be the next queen or something), I would give New Zealand a slogan to share with the world. Have it printed onto the flag. It would say: "New Zealand. Up for anything. Will always make it work". (And if there was enough room, I might add, "And the lamb chops aren't bad either".)

One year later ...

I never intended to share the story of our trip.

The Bog Diaries idea came to me a year after returning home. Completely out of the blue. It was New Year's Eve, and we were housesitting a little ginger cat in Auckland. The four of us. Still together. Just how I like it and how I long for it always to be.

We were sitting around a pine table on a deck under a pergola strung with twinkly warm fairy lights. It was a balmy summer's night, almost eleven thirty.

To help pass the time until midnight, we decided to play a game. The one where everyone has to say what they are grateful for in the year past and what they intend to do with their lives going forward. I love this game. It makes me look cool. It tricks the children into believing I am one of those open-minded mothers who encourage sex before marriage and the use of soft drugs at parties.

Sonny went first.

'Errmm. I'm grateful that I've spent the time learning how to use a camera and making videos, and entertaining people and stuff. I'm going to start my own gaming channel. There's this amazing platform called TikTok that I really think could work for me ....'

Tessa shuffled forward in her seat and rested her elbows on the table.

'I'm grateful that I took my exams early, and I no longer have to do maths. And next year, I want to write more songs and teach myself how to sing soprano. Oh, and I want to learn jazz dancing and become really flexible'.

Brian's turn.

'I'm grateful for the trip that we were able to take last year. How it brought us even closer together as a family .... I will be forever grateful that I have you (looks at kids) as my children and you, Liz (looks at me), as my wife'. *Shit. Sorry, I called you a clean freak, Bri. I didn't mean it. Honest.

After I'd sobbed and heaved and made the night all about me, it was my turn.

'So, what's your dream for next year, Liz?' Brian asked softly.

I sat with my chin in my hand. Looking wistfully into the distance. Like Kylie when Jason dumped her for one of his technicoloured rainbowed cronies.

'I'm going to …' I blinked. 'I'm going to … write a book'.

The tone was dramatic.

Like one might use when announcing to the doctor that they would be forgoing chemotherapy to battle cancer alone in a remote hut somewhere in the Outer Hebrides.

The words took me by surprise.

Where did that come from? A book? Me? This was not pre-planned.

The table fell silent.

'I'm going to write a book about what it was like to … travel the world with … with the best family a woman could ever ask for'. I swallowed. A solitary tear dropped onto my cheek. I waited for the euphoric cheers.

Silence. Muteness. Open-mouthed stares. From everyone.

There was a box of matches on the table. Tessa picked them up and began to crush the sides together. She blinked and placed them down again.

'Wow … well … that's … nice'. She looked from Sonny to Brian and then back to me. Her eyes wide with panic. Her breath grew heavy. Her tone carried caution. She chose her words carefully. 'As long as … well … as long as you don't mention anything … about *us* in it ….' She twisted her thumb around her fingers.

Pfft. Stupid idiotic girl.

If I was the kind of woman who was mature both in years and attitude and bothered to educate herself on the important matters in life, such as human rights and children's privacy requests, I might have said, 'Of course not, darling. I wouldn't dream of it. Anything you say, my angel'.

But I'm not, and I haven't. So I didn't.

'We'll see about that, shall we? Miss clever clogs', I said, swigging wine from my glass and staining my teeth. Then I threw back my head and began to laugh hysterically so that everyone would think it was a joke, and I was the funniest and happiest person who walked the planet and not some psycho lunatic who couldn't control her emotions and cried all the time.

Sonny coughed awkwardly.

Tessa looked horrified.

And Brian wiped the crumbs from the tablecloth into his hands.

ACKNOWLEDGEMENTS

Thank you to Brian, for everything. But especially for this. Without your constant reassurance and strength, I would never have completed this book. You are selfless, kind, genuine, talented, loving, and strong. I knew from the first day, Bri. I knew that you were the one. It was only ever you. It will only ever be you. I love you so very much, darling. You are my world. My everything. My you.

Thank you, Sonny, and Tessa.

Not only for being the best kids in the world, but for being kind and patient, and for letting your mum write exaggerated stories about you on the internet.

Your goodness, loyalty, talent, and maturity fill my heart with so much love, happiness and pride.

You both have a very special gift: the gift of finding humour in every situation. Cherish that gift and don't ever lose it; it will stand by you.

Thank you, Sonny, for being strong and gentle, funny, and wise; all at the same time. Thank you for leading the way in entertainment and for reminding me that I am writing for an audience that deserves it. I love you, bun. So much.

Thank you, Tess, for laughing in all the right places. For the hand-holding, the coffees, and the drives. You are such a good listener, my angel. You light up my life with your you-ness. I love you to the moon and back.

And lastly, to both of you, thank you for coming around the world with me and for not being brats.

Ever.

Thank you to my mum.

For dragging me into the headmaster's office of Newquay Tretherras School when I was sixteen years old and demanding that I be allowed to take my A levels, even though I didn't have the right qualifications and was happy to settle for a secretarial course and then the dole.

Thank you for what you said to me six years ago.

In case you have forgotten, I will remind you. You said, 'Lizzy, put everything else to the side and do what you were put on this earth to do. Write.' This book happened because of you, Mum. You are strong, you are brave, and you are beautiful. I am your princess, and you will always be my queen.

Thank you to Kev.

Your wise words of encouragement and the fact that you laughed at my rubbish doodles gave me the encouragement to continue. Thank you for believing in me and for keeping me on the path. I love you Kev. You can come for Christmas at ours anytime.

Thank you to Hilary, my editor. For being kind but firm, supportive and encouraging. For being cheery, and for delivering far and beyond what I expected. Thank you, Hil. Without you, this book would have no proper punctuation, and the word 'perfect' would be repeated twenty zillion times. You are wonderful and I appreciate you.

Thank you to my friends and family who never complained when all I ever wanted to talk about was 'my book'.

And lastly, thank you to every one of my wonderful newsletter readers, YouTube watchers and podcast listeners.

The people who have been with me from the start; from the day I announced my plans to write this book. I wish I could name you all individually and tell you just how much your loveliness means to me. Your emails, your messages, your never-failing support. You make my little corner of the internet a safe and happy place. I wrote this book in front of you, and because of you. I hope it was worth the wait. Thank you.

Lastly, thank you to Maggie. My girl. My constant companion. Who has slept at my feet and kept me company while I typed. Twitching. Lightly snoring. Sometimes trumping. You are the best dog in the world Mags.

ABOUT THE AUTHOR

Having never written a book before, I wasn't entirely sure what I was supposed to say in this part.

Flicking through other books, it seems that this is the part where I am supposed to say something about myself, like: 'Liz is really good and nice. She is not at all the delusional, emotional schizophrenic woman she portrays in this book. In fact, she's very normal. She loves her children and husband immensely and lives in a house with a roof in New Zealand'.

But that wouldn't be me.

So rather than do what every other best-selling and-knows-far-more-than-me-author has done in the past, I thought I'd go with what's in my heart. And do it my way.

This is the first book I've ever written. Before this, I was a blogger. When I set out to write *The Travel Bog Diaries*, I naively told myself it would be easy. Like blogging, only with an ISBM number.

I thought that all I would have to do to produce a book is take all of my blogging expertise and combine it with my very intelligent and extremely sophisticated writing skills. Bundle it together like one of those rations packages that kids used to carry in the war.

How wrong I was.

Writing this book has been the most emotionally challenging, fabulously brilliant, blood-sloggingly torturous, euphorically delirious, really-bloody-nail-biting thing I have ever done in. my. life. (In fact, you can read all about it soon. *The   Bog Diaries: Writing a Book,* is already underway. Hurray! How's that for a plug?!)

'I'm writing a book, and it will be ready in three months', I bragged to my mum and my thirty-nine friends on Facebook.

Tick …Tock …Tick …Tock …Y …a … w … n … Two and a half two years later…

I compare my book-writing skills to watching paint dry. Fumy, slow, and in need of at least three coats. Two Christmases came and went, and still, no book to gift to my family.

'I'll be nailed up in my box and buried six feet under before you get it published', my mum said encouragingly.

I began to regret telling people about my book-writing plans. So often I wanted to throw the towel in.

'It's too hard', I would wail to Brian more times than I care to admit . 'It just isn't worth it. Top my glass up, Bri. I'm through. I'm rubbish. It's over. I'm done. I QUIT'.

But as you can see, I didn't quit.

Thanks to the unwavering support of those around me, I persevered. Kept going until, eventually, my book and I got into an agreeable groove. Became friends.

Dare I say … fell in love?

I stuck with my book-writing promise. And I'm so glad that I did. Because here it is. The *Travel Bog Diaries*. Forever in print. For you and my mum and my children to read.

While writing this book was the hardest thing I have ever done, the second most challenging thing is what I am about to do now.

Ask you for a review.

Request that you share your thoughts on what you have just read.

You may not know this (I didn't before I began this journey), but when you write a review on a book (be it good, bad or indifferent), that book gets shown and recommended to others.

Don't ask me how this happens. I have no idea. Up until last year, I thought Twitter was a bird shop.

Being a British scaredy-cat who would rather stick her fingers in her ears and sing, 'Lah, lah, lah, don't care, can't hear you', than ask for your thoughts on my work, asking for a review isn't easy.

But I'm going to be brave and do it anyway.

Because while asking for a review is hard, spending two years of my life slumped over a computer stuck in a never-ending teenage time warp and knowing no one will ever read my book is much harder!

Before I leave you to run around the garden with my knickers on my head, I would like to say thank you.

Thank you for taking the trip with us around the world. It was a pleasure having you. And thank you for finding it in your heart to write a review and share a few words about my book. If you go to www.thetravelbogdiaries.com/review/ it will lead you directly to the book's Amazon page where you can leave a review.

Brian, Sonny, Tessa, and I will read every single message and review, that's a promise.

And don't forget: *More Travel Bog Diaries (Book 2)* is available to pre-order now on Amazon! Yippee!!

That's right, there are lots more *Travel Bog Diary* entries to share! Find out all about what happened in Hong Kong after the bowel problems, read about the alcoholic aristocrat that we house-sat for in Ireland, and discover why Tessa had to sleep in a rabbit hutch in Florence…Pre-order *More Travel Bog Diaries (Book 2)* now!

Until we meet again, my friend, Bon Voyage! And remember: Life is an adventure. Now, go out and have yours!

Liz x

PS: I didn't include it in this book as the word count was already massive but I have a "hidden chapter". One that I am yet to share. This chapter is the *very* first entry of the Travel Bog Diaries. Written from the USA in the first week of our big adventure. It's brilliant. Very raw and honest and written (of course) from the bog.

As a way of saying thank you for supporting me and for sharing a review, I would like to gift that diary entry to you. Look on it as a secret, yet-to-be-revealed treat!

To access the hidden diary entry, go to www.thetravelbogdiaries.com/hiddenchapter and I will happily send it to you. It's hilarious, you will love it! And don't worry, I have the kids' permission. They were asleep when I asked them but I think that still counts.

PPS: Liz lives in New Zealand with her family, her dog and her two sheep.

You can connect with Liz by signing up to her free lengthy newsletter. In it she shares photos of her kids that she hasn't got permission to do, and other stuff that's quite good.

www.lizdeacle.com

Subscribe to Liz and Brian's popular comedy podcast, *It's a Drama!* Where they share down-to-earth intimate conversations about midlife, world travel, relationships and family. Sometimes, Liz drags Sonny and Tessa to the mic too. Find our podcast on your favourite podcasting app or head to:

www.itsadrama.com/podcast

Printed in Great Britain
by Amazon

47556765R00148